Endorsement

Addictions have become one of the top problems in today's North America. Almost every family has at least one addicted member. How do we as believers assist true seekers in finding freedom? Dr. Douglas and Pamela Carr not only layout the problem but describe in detail the steps to freedom. They noted the characteristics of the octopus and used it to frame the addiction challenges, outlining each issue and the route to freedom. I know both Doug and Pam well. I have watched them blossom over the years we have been in relationship. They started with healing and delivering themselves of their own issues and broke through into helping others. Now they are flourishing. I highly recommend both them and this book.

Barbara J Yoder

Lead Apostle
Shekinah Regional Apostolic Center
Breakthrough Apostolic Ministries Network
www.shekinahchurch.org
www.barbaraYODERblog.com

BREAKING
THE OCTOPUS GRIP OF
ADDICTION

DR. DOUGLAS E. CARR

WESTBOW
PRESS®
A DIVISION OF THOMAS NELSON
& ZONDERVAN

WestBow Press books may be ordered through booksellers or by contacting:

WestBow Press
A Division of Thomas Nelson & Zondervan
1663 Liberty Drive
Bloomington, IN 47403
www.westbowpress.com
1 (866) 928-1240

Cover and Sketches by Barbara De Simon; Creative Director of ROOTED Publishing

ISBN: 978-1-9736-8451-0 (sc)
ISBN: 978-1-9736-8453-4 (hc)
ISBN: 978-1-9736-8452-7 (e)

Library of Congress Control Number: 2020901491

Print information available on the last page.

WestBow Press rev. date: 01/27/2020

CONTENTS

ACKNOWLEDGMENTS

Holy Spirit is the life and breath behind everything good I write. I personally take responsibility for anything not good or edifying. Something special happened to me at the Strike the Match meeting with Chuck Pierce, Dutch and Tim Sheets, and Barbara Yoder on December 9, 2018, in Flint Michigan. That meeting shifted things in Pam and me, our region, and in states and nations connected with Breakthrough Apostolic Ministries Network.

On Monday, December 17, 2018, the Lord shared one result of that shift in my Daily Listening Room where I record what I sense He shares with me. This is what I recorded. *Son, I gave you three sermons last week! I gave you most of a fourth one on Saturday when you sat down to rest with the computer on your lap for three hours. Last week, while you watched a movie, I gave you the outline of Breaking the Octopus Grip of Addiction. I have given you Pamela and her willingness to help you write this book. I AM speaking, as I always have, but you have moved into a season of greater listening and I have assigned a Scribe Angel to you, so things will come more quickly to you. Your major assignment for 2019 and beyond is writing. Your second greatest assignment is equipping His House Church for greatness. Your third greatest assignment is equipping of deliverance ministers. Your marriage and family are not an assignment but a covenant you must always keep. I AM with you this day. Enjoy!* I responded, "Thank you, Father." And He said, *"This is abundance!"*

Therefore, I acknowledge Holy Spirit first and foremost. Without Him, my words would be simply human. I pray He helps you separate what He is speaking to you personally, from anything I have written on my own.

I am grateful for my precious wife of over twenty-five years! I am thrilled God put it on her heart to share her story and insight concerning addiction and how it affects addicts *and* their families. Pam is a great worshipper and listener. She has learned thriving is so much better than striving. Her walk with the Lord makes that possible.

Suzanne LeBlanc continues to support us and lend her critical eye to what we write. She notices things little and large that need adjusting. She also provides priceless help with formatting, pagination and the like.

In July of 2019, I hoped this book would be completed during 2019, but something was missing. God revealed the missing piece in perfect timing. Pam and I attended a Barbie Breathitt Dreams and Visions Conference at Shekinah Regional Apostolic Center on the second weekend of July 2019. Pam is a seer, I am not. I take comfort in the words of Jesus to Thomas when He said, "Because you have seen me, you have believed; blessed are those who have not seen and yet have believed." (John 20:29)

Those gifted to see, saw things I only long to look into. They reported seeing angels, heavenly mists, and the like in the sanctuary. Even though I didn't see what they did, I benefited greatly by the conference and was thankful for what Barbie imparted into our lives.

Pam bought some of Barbie's materials, including a dictionary of symbols seen in dreams and visions. I never thought I would use it, but a few days later a friend called me and mentioned seeing an octopus over someone she was praying for. She suggested I look it up in a prophetic dictionary. I was moved to look for the definition of octopus in Barbie's book. I was taken back when I read her entry, for it describes the scope of *Breaking the Octopus Grip of Addiction*. Therefore, I acknowledge Barbie for her quote below.

> **Octopus:** the diabolical spirit of Jezebel that entangles other people; operates with a strong spirit of control and manipulation. Deceptive lies

that slander and destroy a person's reputation, inflicts confusion that causes despair and depression; a spirit of murder that leads to the victim comp templating suicide.[1]

I gratefully acknowledge Barbara De Simon for her help and for designing the cover and the graphics for the Octopus.

She is Creative Director of ROOTED Publishing and author of *Barren NO MORE*[2] and K*ey to Fertility*[3]. I appreciate her/ but don't see her often. I was amazed when she emailed me after my book *Making Abundance a Lifestyle Rather than an Event*[4] was released. She congratulated me and offered to develop a book cover for me. I mentioned this book, and she developed its incredible cover. I then asked her about drawing the octopus, complete with pictures of one tentacle being severed twice from the body after each section is dealt with.

Barbara asked how the tentacles should be labeled and in what order. I hadn't given much thought to this, but when she asked, my mind thought "from far-left to far-right and in that order until the each is removed." Sensing my mind was getting in the way, I asked my wife about it and she saw it slashing from left to right. Still questioning what God wanted, I asked Pam to pray about it while I jumped in the shower.

I was barely wet before I had the novel thought of asking God. He confirmed what Pam sensed. Later that morning, I asked God about how He wanted the tentacles cut off. I was in my Daily Listening Room (where I journal when I sense the Lord is speaking to me). God revealed His answer: *This morning you asked about the order of cutting the tentacles off the octopus and I immediately answered: "cut them off from the left side because so doing will cause the octopus to begin veering to the left making it much harder to hit its target." This little bit of revelation opens up many things for you and for the book.*

The members of His House Church understand and encourage God's call on my life to write, serve the larger church as an apostle of deliverance, and network with others for transformation. They lovingly support Pam and me in all we do.

Finally, I am indebted to people who struggle with addictions and trust us with their struggles. Their parents and spouses also give great insight by relating how challenging the addiction(s) of family members are to each and every member of the family.

Endnotes:

1   Dr. Barbie L Breathitt, *A to Z Dream Symbology Dictionary*, page 306, Second Printing. Copyright 2017-Barbie Breathitt Enterprises. All rights reserved.
2   Barbara De Simon, *Barren No More: From Barrenness to Fruitfulness*. 2017 ROOTED Publishing for Kindle Direct Print.
3   Barbara De Simon, *Key to Fertility: Healing Stress and Hidden Fears That Could Be Hindering Fertility*. Barbara De Simon, February 21, 2019, sold by Smashwords.
4   Dr. Douglas E. Carr, *Making Abundance a Lifestyle Rather Than an Event*. Kindle Direct Print, July 16, 2019.

FOREWORD

Recovery. Such an inspiring word, full of hope and optimism. A word surrounded by positivity. Sadly, in our day, this is an all too needed word. After reading Douglas Carr's book, *Breaking the Octopus Grip of Addiction*, and being a Christian in recovery for over 28 years, I recognize the spiritual tools this book can provide for those in, and those searching for recovery, as well as for the church as a whole.

It took me many years to see and understand how most of my personal battles, especially in the beginning stages of recovery were spiritual in nature, and that I was in need of biblical solutions in order to "recover." Today, I oversee a ministry for the Lord and have helped thousands of people through a Christ-centered recovery program. I will be grateful to have this book as a weapon against spiritual attacks for our members.

I see *Breaking the Octopus Grip of Addiction* as a great reference tool that would have been a helpful spiritual weapon for me early on in my own recovery. I believe it is God's answer for people suffering from addiction today. The most common question I hear from church members who struggle with addiction/ or those who have a family member, friend or fellow church member, suffering from addiction is "What do I do next?" I believe this book, along with spiritual guidance from the church body, is a great start. I pray in Jesus' Name; this book will open up an avenue for discussion that will cause breakthroughs for anyone who holds it in their hands.

Randy Leviton,
Director, Damascus Road Ministry
damascusroadmi.org
62 Division St, Coldwater, MI 49036

AUTHORS' PREFACE

I (Doug) began crying out to God for this book because of frustration and disappointment. No person, parent, pastor or deliverance minister wants to see continuing failure, especially when it hits people they love and care for.

I think of individuals whose loving parents have done everything possible to set them on the right track. They are charming people, young and old, bubbling over with potential. They have dreams of being great evangelists, pastors, worship leaders, etc. Many have a call to touch hundreds of people for the Kingdom of God. Unfortunately, addictive behavior continues to compel many into harmful behaviors that pull them away from their prophetic destinies, landing many in jail or prison.

Too many serve their time, are released from jail and get off to a good start for a while, but often break parole and end up back in jail. Countless individuals may spend most of their lives in jail unless we intervene. We need further revelation to break Satan's hold through addiction over their lives.

Many parents of addicts are in ministry and faithfully serve Jesus. Their children have received powerful prophetic words concerning how God wants to use them. Their intelligence is often far above normal, and God has plans to prosper them and give them a hope and a future. When my wife Pam and I meet them, we immediately take a liking to them and sense God has great plans for them.

Some come around and find freedom after one or two appointments. Many, however, take three steps forward and then the enemy knocks them back two steps through addictive behavior. Thank God for the testimonies many have developed. God truly works miracles in some addicts. Praise God for every victory. But we will need to continue crying out to God on their behalf because we know how powerful addiction can be.

There are individuals with great ability to memorize and quote Scripture. When they are clean, they have the anointing to minister powerfully. They've led many to salvation and deliverance through their ministries. They have great potential IF they get clean and stay clean. It is no wonder the enemy is so vigilant in using addiction to knock them back time and again! The devil loves a shiny mark.

Many parents of addicts are godly and strong intercessors, yet their adult children keep getting into trouble. I've prayed with many who now walk in freedom, but my heart cries out for everyone who falls back into bondage. If they start ignoring my calls and texts, I know where they are headed. Time and again they end up back in jail. We continue crying out for their total release from bondage. I trust and believe God is giving answers many are seeking for, which makes this book a work of faith.

I've written dozens of letters to incarcerated addicts. I've written some weekly. I 've sent my sermons to many, and they say they appreciate them. They promise in good faith to stay clean when they are released. Unfortunately, at least up to this point, the devil has used strong addictions to repeatedly pull many who are determined to break free back into addiction.

There are several good and helpful recovery plans. I appreciate Celebrate Recovery so much I helped initiate its program in two county jails near where we live. Praise God for everyone who has broken free of addiction and is moving forward into their God-given destiny! But, I can't, I won't be satisfied until we have God's revelation to see the "tough cases" set free.

I believe the Great I Am is releasing the revelation we need. Godly parents and grandparents have been crying out to God for years on behalf of addicts. I've joined them in recent years and began publicly requesting prayer for answers several months ago.

The day before I began writing this book, we watched the full-length movie *The Heart of Christmas* during our normal two-hour worship service. My wife and I had previewed it a few days earlier. It is a riveting movie, so I was surprised when God downloaded a vision of the "octopus of addiction" and then labeled each tentacle that works under the strongman through the stronghold of The Root Spirit of Bondage. (also called "Spirit of Bondage)

This brings great hope! Another wonderful addition to this book is my wife, Pamela, co-authoring it with me! She experienced her Father's addictions and addictive behavior from her birth until he died much younger than he might have apart from addiction.

As many already know, the death of an addicted parent does not break the hold of ancestral addiction off their descendants.

CO-AUTHOR PAM'S PREFACE

I (Pam) had very good parents. We didn't have a lot of extras, but we always had enough.

I knew my dad smoked but that was about all I knew. I didn't know smoking was an addiction, I simply thought it was his choice.

I was very close to my dad, so I never saw anything wrong in him or his behavior. I can still smell cigar smoke from the times we went to the bowling alley together. They were special times for me, so the smell of smoke has never bothered me. I did have to clean the ashtrays, and I didn't enjoy that very much but the smell was never offensive to me.

When I was a teenager, my dad took a job far from home and commuted home on the weekends. During the week he'd go to the local bar with his new work buddies and soon started drinking too much. I still didn't know this was a problem. Most of the time, my dad was quite funny when he drank, he rarely became mean when drinking.

As I grew older, even though I didn't smoke or drink, things started to surface in my life. I couldn't make plans. I was insecure. I tried to fix things in other people's lives. The list goes on and on . . .

To make a long story short, in the late eighties, I was seeing a counselor because I *had* messed up my own life. After several sessions, I found out that my dad was an alcoholic and I was an adult child of an alcoholic.

I was furious with my mother because she didn't tell me. Perhaps she thought I should have figured it out for myself, but I didn't. I really felt like I had been deceived. I went straight to her house and confronted her. We had a long talk about things that had happened while I was growing up.

My way of life felt shattered and I didn't know what to do. I remember being on my knees, not because I was spiritual, but because I was drying my hair and only had one plug receptacle that would work. I think that was the first time I cried out to God. I remember, asking Him where He was, and that all I had ever tried to do was to find Him. In the most gentle voice, I've ever heard, He answered and said, "Look Up." I saw a maze that was over my head. I was caught in it and if I looked to Him, He would lead me through.

I began to understand why dad had placed the blame on mom. I began to understand why I behaved the way I did. When I started to seek the Lord about this, He said "I didn't reveal this to you so you can use it as an excuse. I revealed this to you so you can overcome it!"

By this time, I was addicted to tobacco and could have easily turned to alcohol because of things going on in my own life.

DOUG'S WRAP UP OF OUR PREFACE

On Sunday morning, 12/16/2018, we showed the movie *The Heart of Christmas* produced by Andrew Wommack Ministries. I always meet with my prayer partners at 9:30 on Sunday mornings. That particular morning, I asked them to pray for me to receive revelation from heaven, so we can help others break strongholds of addiction that torment so many families like those mentioned earlier.

Even though Pam and I previewed the entire movie the week before, I figured I would watch the movie again, this time on "the big screen" at our church. I was moved, however, at the last minute to grab a nine-page article I wanted to read through.

What actually happened, however, was God moved me to use the back pages of the article to record as He downloaded the Octopus head, then named the head and each tentacle during the opening part of the movie. This book is the result of fleshing out the revelation God gave that day. Praise be to God! May HIS insights be a blessing for you and yours and all in need of freedom from addiction.

CHAPTER ONE

OVERVIEW

Sketch by Barbara De Simon; Creative
Director of ROOTED Publishing.

I (Pam) have always looked at addiction like a ball of tangled up yarn. When you start to untangle it, you often find another color knotted up with the one you are trying to unravel. This can go on multiple times depending on what you are dealing with. I think the most important thing to do is find a starting point to unravel that which is a tangled-up mess. The same is true of addiction.

Addiction can be like a form of cancer. If you look at the head of the octopus as where addiction exists in your mind, Satan will use one of the eight tentacles and cause it to grow. Depending on how long you have struggled, the tentacle grows in length and strength. Some tentacles may not be very long, but like a short piece of yarn tangled in a ball, Satan tangles the "tentacles" to where even the short ones make it harder to unravel, holding people in agreement with Satan's assignment, holding them in bondage.

I believe when you have all eight tentacles working, you

have come into agreement with the one who wants to kill, steal and destroy.

The fact is, we have been created in the image of God. We have His DNA. We also have Satan's image that looks like this octopus, and it will continue to grow if allowed to. Unfortunately, most of us become entangled before we realize what is happening.

God gave me (Doug) a revelation of an octopus with eight tentacles, that we quickly outline in this overview.

The Head Represents the Root Spirit of Bondage.

📖 For you did not receive *the spirit of bondage* again to fear, but you received the Spirit of adoption by whom we cry out, "Abba, Father." (Romans 8:15, NKJV, emphasis mine).

This root spirit is assigned to hold people in bondage in various ways, most notably, addiction. We will look at it further in Chapter 3 after we consider the nature of Octopi in Chapter 2, where we give an overview of the octopus structure of addiction and its tentacles.

Rejection is the devil's reaction to Holy Spirit conviction for us to forgive those who hurt us, in order to open a path to receive healing from deep inner wounds. The cure for rejection begins with a difficult, but necessary choice to forgive others from the point of the offense. That is a prerequisite to receiving Jesus' healing of broken hearts as outlined in Luke 4:18 and Isaiah 61.

Consider how Jesus began to summarize Isaiah 61 in Luke 4:18–19,

📖 "The Spirit of the LORD *is* upon Me, Because He has anointed Me To preach the gospel to *the* poor; He has sent Me to heal the brokenhearted, To proclaim liberty to *the* captives And recovery of sight to *the* blind, *To* set at liberty those who are

oppressed; To proclaim the acceptable year of the LORD."
(Luke 4:18-19, NKJV)

The opposite of rejection is acceptance of God's presence, love, compassion, and healing from past and present hurt. This can be accomplished by asking Holy Spirit to take you back to the incident that instigated the pain and trauma. He can open your book of memories, show you where God was and what He was doing during times of trauma, and lead you into deep healing of inner wounds.

I (Pam) believe rejection is something we are all born with. We have all inherited rejection from our first ancestors: Adam and Eve brought rejection upon us all through their disobedience. They are the ones who introduced sin into our lives in the first place. God didn't reject Adam, but He had to separate Himself from Adam and Eve because of sin. God rejected Satan, not us.

Satan wants to keep us from finding our covering, (Jesus) in order to keep us in bondage to rejection.

Iniquity is both personal and ancestral. Iniquity is literally a bent, twisting, or distortion of character that is passed through human blood and/or legal ancestry. Legal ancestry includes adoption, stepparents, godparents, and the like. The opposite of iniquity includes being renewed through the blood from Jesus' bruises in order to receive Abba Father's DNA. Pam inserted a thoughtful question at this point. She asked: "Do you think we have the Father's DNA because of being created in His image? I know we have a sinful nature but isn't that what we are supposed to overcome?"

"Good question, Pam!" We are created in God's image, but personal and ancestral iniquity has distorted His image in us. When we are born again, however, we are born again of His imperishable seed (In the Greek the word is 'Sperma,' from that we get the English word *'sperm.'*) In other words, we take on God's DNA when we are born again!

Pam adds, "I knew I had brown hair, emphasis on *'had,'* when I was younger, and I looked a little like mom and a little like dad, but I had no idea I would be drawn into the same iniquitous patterns as my parents."

We do inherit things good and bad from our ancestors, but everything from our heavenly Father is good. We pray God will use this book to help people become free from everything negative inherited from earthly parents and grasp hold of everything positive inherited from our Father in Heaven.

THE THIRD TENTACLE IS REBELLION

Rebellion can be personal, ancestral, and/or demonic. Rebellion can be defined as an act of violent or open resistance to an established government or rule and is easily recognized in every level of today's society. But rebellion goes deeper, and at its core, it insists on personal rights and gratification. I wrote in *Choosing Kingdom*[1] how the devil set the prototype of rebellion with his five "I wills" where he disregarded God's authority and tried to make himself God. Jesus, on the other hand, set the prototype of the Kingdom of God by saying "Nonetheless, not my will, but thine be done."

The opposite of rebellion is full abandonment and submission to God through Jesus' sweat drops of shed blood in Gethsemane.

In the Garden of Eden, Adam and Eve followed Lucifer's prototype, basically telling God "Not thy will, but ours be done."

Jesus, being incarnate as fully God and human, was tempted in every way such as we are. In the Garden of Gethsemane, Jesus was tempted to resist God's will for Him to be the perfect sacrificial lamb and pay humankind's full penalty for sin on the cross. He repeatedly prayed, "Father, if it possible remove this cup from me." Each time Jesus prayed thus, He added, "Nonetheless, not my will but thine be done." Luke's Gospel records how Jesus shed drops of blood the last time He prayed that. We can apply the blood Jesus shed in Gethsemane to break the curse of rebellion and narcissism and release the blessing of total abandonment to God. (For more information, check out *From Woe Is Me Io Wow Is He!* Chapter 3.)[2]

Pam astutely notes: "It seems like one of the first words we learn as a child is the meaning of "no!" "That is where the battle of the wills begins."

THE FOURTH TENTACLE IS PYTHON AND/OR SORCERY

We will consider important steps to be taken here, making it possible to align with the Lord so He will rebuke the devourer who preys on addictive behavior.

The way the hold of python and sorcery manifests in addictive behavior can be illustrated by being trapped in quicksand. Once you open the doors and step in, addiction will suck you in before you realize it. Hidden behaviors grip the addict, things like using in secret, lying, denying reality, trying to hide from God, and the like begin manifesting through cooperation with other spirits like python, sorcery, and addiction.

Addicts often have fragmented parts (alters or parts of themselves broken off their core) which were broken off and disconnected through pain and trauma. Therefore, addicts learn to seek comfort through substance abuse rather than through the Holy Spirit Who is The Paraclete and Comforter sent from Abba Father.

Jesus left His peace for believers to enjoy. A soul that has one or more tears (rips) in it, however, doesn't have His peace, at least not in the broken pieces. Many, if not most, addictions mask inner pain a person feels. Satan makes people believe addiction is a way of escape from pain.

THE SIXTH TENTACLE IS TRAUMA

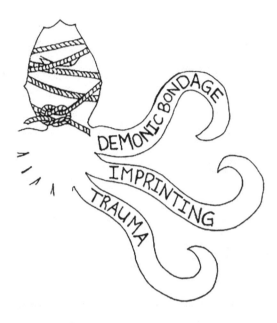

Trauma usually comes through things warring against one's body and soul. It may be a conflict with parents, siblings, or abusive relatives or friends. Veterans of wars, especially the Vietnam War and the Persian Gulf War, are subject to trauma that may hold them in bondage to addiction. Pam adds, "I believe blame and excuses also manifest here."

THE SEVENTH TENTACLE IS IMPRINTING

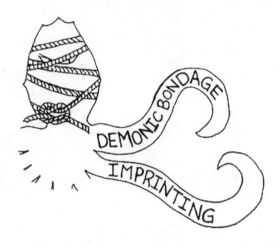

Imprinting comes through family, friends, music, television, Internet and role models. It can also come through demonic voices and delusions, including demonic, emotional, or mental delusion. Such delusions mask personal identity and the image of God in people.

I thought of the story of the "ugly duckling," here. In reality, it was a swan cygnet (baby swan) who felt out of place and rejected because it was raised with ducks. Many addicts struggle with imprinting, from family members or friends, contrary to their spiritual nature.

Pam says, "Faith and self-confidence/self-worth is damaged by the tentacle of imprinting." I hadn't thought of that before, but she is right. Imprinting lures people to emulate others, and rather than discovering and developing their own identities, they let the imprint of others determine who they become, rather than discovering whom God made them to be.

THE FINAL TENTACLE IS DEMONIC BONDAGE AND ASSIGNMENTS

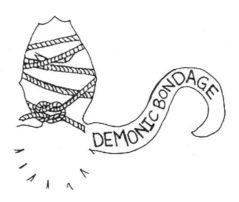

Each of these tentacles is like a wire of the cable Satan wants to use to bind individuals. If such things are not dealt with, hopelessness usually sets in. Hopelessness is the opposite of the faith needed to break free.

God chooses and appoints people even before they are born. The truth God spoke to Jeremiah applies to each person. God has a chosen plan for every person. The plan varies for each individual, but God has a blueprint to bless each one.

📖 "Before I formed you in the womb I knew you; Before you were born I sanctified you; I ordained you a prophet to the nations." (Jeremiah 1:5, NKJV)

Addicts and their families sometimes blame God for their problems, as if He wills for them to continually struggle. Nothing could be further from the truth. I wrote *Schematics ~ God's Blueprint versus Satan's Programming*[3] because people often need greater clarity of the three great influencers in their life. There is God, (whom some addicts refer to as their Higher

Power); the devil, whom Jesus said is the thief that comes to kill, steal and destroy; and finally, the individual. Contrary to much secular and religious thinking, each person has the greatest responsibility for how his or her life turns out. In other words, "the buck stops with each individual." Early in the morning when I began doing this revision, I texted a friend who has struggled with addiction. I wrote "Well (name withheld), you have been out of corrections for three Sundays and in church only one time out of three. Just how serious are you about following Christ? I continue praying for you but neither God nor the devil has the greatest impact on your life. Only you have the choice of whether to make your life all it can be, or not! Choose this day whom you will serve. Praying for you right now."

The ball is in his court. He can choose to respond or ignore my text of concern. He can choose whether to follow Jesus and His perfect will for his life or give in to Satan's continuing attempt to derail his life. That is why it is important to realize that even though God wants to help, and Satan wants to destroy, each individual is solely responsible for his or her choices.

During twenty-five years of deep healing and deliverance ministry, I have witnessed how the devil and his demons have assignments to hinder people from fulfilling their prophetic destinies. As Paul indicates, we need to take responsibility for our prophetic destinies.

  📖 For we are His workmanship, created in Christ Jesus for good works, which God prepared beforehand that *we should walk in them.* (Ephesians 2:10, NKJ V, emphasis mine)

I am absolutely convinced the devil works hardest against those who are destined to be greatly used by the Lord.

The vision God gave me (Doug) for this book is the need to first bind the strongman of bondage and tear down its stronghold. From there we will deal with eight specific satanic assignments leading to further entrapment by addiction. Each of these assignments has a ruling demon bent on bringing death and destruction to those under its control, as represented by tentacles of the octopus.

As we address each tentacle, we will do a double cutting it off and then forbid it to regenerate. We will address each tentacle in turn, and once we have dealt with each of them, the strongman of bondage will have lost its footing and will be easily cast out.

Dr. Luke gives important insight concerning binding the strongman and dealing with the plunder he has stolen from people. He teaches us to first bind the strongman in the Name of Jesus. Christians may not understand it, but in Christ, they are stronger than the strongman and can overtake him.

📖 But if I cast out demons with the finger of God, surely the kingdom of God has come upon you. When a strong man, fully armed, guards his own palace, his goods are in peace. But when a stronger than he comes upon him and overcomes him, he takes from him all his armor in which he trusted, and divides his spoils (or plunder). (Luke 11:20-22, NKJV)

In Jesus, we are stronger than the strongman! Following Jesus' instructions, we will bind the strongman and take away his armor (here illustrated as tentacles that are also called "arms") Once we do that, we can take back what the enemy has plundered from people, and help each one truly experience the fullness of his or her prophetic destiny and God-given design. God's desire is for each one to walk in victory and enjoy life more abundantly.

It is our hope believers will use the steps outlined in *Breaking Addiction's Octopus Grip* to find personal freedom and then minister the same to others in need.

We will explain this step by step after you have the opportunity to meet the octopus.

Endnotes:

1   Dr. Douglas E. Carr, *Choosing Kingdom*, Create Space, 2017.
2   Dr. Douglas E. Carr, *From Woe Is Me to Wow Is He!* Chapter 2, *Tale of Two Gardens*, Create Space, 2016.
3   Dr. Douglas E. Carr, *Schematics ~ God's Blueprint versus Satan's Programming*, Create Space 2014.

CHAPTER TWO

MEET THE OCTOPUS

Octopi (plural of octopus, also called octopuses) are strange and amazing creatures. Several of their characteristics illustrate the work of addictions, as well as demonic assignments and bondages.

One example is their ability to rapidly alter their shape, which enables them to squeeze through small gaps, such as the shell of a mollusk. Likewise, addiction and any demons associated with it can squeeze through small gaps in an addict. They can squeeze the tip of a tentacle through a crack in the addict's soul and take full control of a person. For instance, if an addict has even a tiny amount of unforgiveness, or a little bit of self-hatred, or an area of rejection, etc., addictions and/ or demons can work their way in. Octopi can also change color, even as addictive substances do. Addictive substances promise to be comforting friends but end up being horrible slaveholders.

Another telling characteristic octopi share with addicts is they have complex nervous systems, excellent sight, and are among the most intelligent and behaviorally diverse of all invertebrates. Many addicts are incredibly intelligent - at least until their mental functions are debilitated by addiction. An addict's behavior may vary within individuals. At times they may be loving and kind, and then suddenly turn hateful and cruel.

Third, most species of octopi are venomous and can bite their prey, injecting it with poison, though only the blue-ringed octopus is usually deadly to humans. Addicts often spew their poison on people who care most for them: harsh words, abusive or demanding behavior, theft and the like. Addictive substances are like poison. At first, addictions are more harmful than deadly. Prolonged use of many drugs, including tobacco, alcohol, illegal and prescribed drugs, etc., often leads to premature death. I watched my own mother struggle for her last breath after forty-odd years of nicotine addiction. She died just before she and my Father were to begin the retirement they so looked forward to and planned for many years. Their dreams were shattered through my mother's early death by addiction.

Octopi have hard beaks for tearing the flesh of their prey apart to devour it. Addictions tear the flesh of their victims. Opioids and crystal meth are two of the most damaging addictions I've worked with. Many become addicted after their first use. The venom of addiction brings continuous and compulsive use, despite evidence of how harmful it is. I served on the St. Joseph County Meth Task Force for several years. I witnessed many once beautiful people whose appearance and lives were destroyed by the scourge of meth addiction. Our county judges testify the most common reason children are removed from their homes is parental addiction, especially to Meth.

Octopi have arms lined with powerful suckers for grabbing prey. Anyone who works with addicts knows how addictions suck people into their powerful arms and hold them in bondage. I saw a sad but true bumper sticker that said, "cancer cures smoking." It was lung cancer that made it so my mother could not smoke anymore. That same cancer took her life five months after it was diagnosed. My wife, Pam, shares the following concerning how addictive behavior took her Father:

My dad passed away when he was 45. He also had lung cancer, but he lived with it for two years. He had half of his lung removed and had radiation treatments. Oncologists had just begun using chemo at that time. I am grateful for the years I had with my Father, but sorry his life was so quickly snuffed out as a result of his addiction. I think an important thing to mention here is "Satan is a liar!" We all know that, but when he feeds us those lies, we tend to believe them.

There are warning signs for an addict. Most smokers, for example, develop a cough or shortness of breath. These warning signs are easy to ignore when we believe lies coming in our direction. One lie responds to the fear of being addicted by the thought, "I'm not an addict, I can quit anytime I put my mind to it." The fact is, it is much easier to continue in addiction than it is to overcome it. One's addiction truly becomes their lifestyle.

The powerful sucker I believed was, "if I get addicted to cigarettes, I could quit along with my first husband." He had told me it was too hard to quit, all while I was watching my dad die. I thought my reason for starting to smoke made perfect sense.

One thing I didn't plan on was enjoying smoking, and

believing it helped me to relax. Another lie I believed was that I was only hurting myself, that was not true.

Thank you, Pam, for sharing your heart and insight above! Octopuses can squirt dark ink that clouds the water to confuse predators while the octopus escapes. Anyone who has struggled with addiction or helped others who have can see how the enemy veils the hope and glorious light of the Gospel that can set them free. Many addicts lose all hope and any sense of destiny. Disappointment rises to destroy all their dreams and goals.

The final, and perhaps strongest example of how octopi and additions relate to one another is what happens when their arms (tentacles) are cut off. Severed octopus tentacles have a mind of their own. They continue operating even after they are cut off. An octopus arm may try to pick up food to feed a phantom mouth up to an hour after it is cut off from the body. Even worse, tentacles can regenerate. Within one hundred days after a tentacle is severed, an arm tip will grow back to resemble the original one.

In a similar manner, people who have walked free of addictions for weeks or months may fall back into them overnight. It is as if they have a new arm to reach for a drink, a pill, a morsel, a magazine or whatever else might feed their addiction.

The picture God gave me for this book is to bind the strongman of addiction and tear down the stronghold. Then we will deal with eight specific satanic assignments that have strengthened the strongman's entrapment of bondage. Each of these assignments, represented by tentacles of the octopus, has a ruling demon bent on bringing death and destruction to those it enslaves.

As each tentacle of the octopus is dealt with specifically, it will be cut off twice and forbidden to regenerate. We will also address any demons working through each tentacle. Once all eight tentacles have been addressed, the strongman of bondage will have lost its footing and will be easily cast out.

CHAPTER THREE

THE HEAD OF THE OCTOPUS -

The Root Spirit of Bondage

The head, or strongman, of addiction, is The Root Spirit of Bondage. I included this in my book *Free Indeed from Root Spirits.*[1] That book discusses fifteen spirits identified by name in the Scriptures, plus the root spirit of death. Rather than fully rewrite it for this chapter, I submit a revised version of chapter 2 of this book below.

The Root Spirit of Bondage (Addictive Behaviors)

📖 For ye received not the spirit of bondage again unto fear; but ye received the spirit of adoption, whereby we cry, Abba, Father. (Romans 8:15, ASV)

📖 For freedom did Christ set us free: stand fast therefore, and be not entangled again in a yoke of bondage. (Galatians 5:1, ASV)

The Root Spirit of Bondage is a work of the flesh (Galatians 5:19-21). The fruit of The Root Spirit of Bondage is imprisonment to the devil, addiction, fear, and dishonesty. Because addictions are so – ADDICTIVE – I share a few other important Scriptural insights for your enlightenment.

📖 They promise these people freedom, but they themselves are slaves to corruption. A person is a slave to whatever he gives in to. (2 Peter 2:19, Names of God Bible)

📖 His own iniquities entrap the wicked himself, and he is snared in the cords of his sins. (Proverbs 5:22, MEV)

📖 Jesus answered them, "Most assuredly, I say to you, whoever commits sin is a slave of sin.' (John 8:34, NKJV)

📖 And *that* they may come to their senses *and escape* the snare of the devil, having been taken captive by him to *do* his will. (2 Timothy 2:26, NKJV)

📖 Do you not know that to whom you yield yourselves as slaves to obey, you are slaves of the one whom you obey, whether of sin leading to death, or of obedience leading to righteousness? (Romans 6:16, MEV)

📖 But I see another law in my members, warring against the law of my mind, and bringing me into captivity to the law of sin which is in my members. (Romans 7:23, NKJV)

📖 Then they sailed to the country of the Gadarenes, which is opposite Galilee. And when He stepped out on the land, there met Him a certain man from the city who had demons for a long time. And he wore no clothes, nor did he live in a house but in the tombs. When he saw Jesus, he cried out, fell down before Him, and with a loud voice said, "What have I to do with You, Jesus, Son of the Most High God? I beg You, do not torment me!" For He had commanded the unclean spirit to come out of the man. For it had often seized him, and he was kept under guard, bound with chains and shackles; and he broke the bonds and was driven by the demon into the wilderness. (Luke 8:26-29, NKJV)

📖 For I see that you are poisoned by bitterness and bound by iniquity." (Acts 8:23, NKJV)

Each of the previous verses shows how sin and addiction can hold people captive. A few manifestations of The Spirit of Bondage include captivity to the devil, compulsive sin, bondage to sin and addiction, fear of death, and slave of corruption.

There are various kinds of bondage. We usually think of things like addictions to alcohol and drugs, but other addictions include anorexia, workaholic, and addictions to computers, video games, sex, etc. Codependency is also a strong delusion operating under The Root Spirit of Bondage.

With codependence, there are strong rescuers who "need" someone to rescue, and weak victims who "need" someone to rescue them. They are convinced they cannot live without the other. There are some cultures where the wife is burned to death on husband's funeral pyre (a pile of wood a corpse is burned on, as part of a funeral ceremony in some traditions) if he dies first!

Any behavior a person does not have mastery over might be evidence that The Spirit of Bondage is at work.

The first step in dealing with an area of bondage is to bind the strongman (ruling spirit) over that area, that can be done through the following prayer.

Pray, resist, believe and declare:

\ Father, in Jesus' Mighty Name and through His blood I pray Your protection over me, over those I love and over all who are or will be in this place where I will receive freedom from The Spirit of Bondage.
\ In Jesus' Name, I bind The Strongman Spirit of Bondage.
\ In Jesus' Name, and through His authority I demolish the stronghold of bondage and tear it down with great violence.
\ The weapons of my warfare are not carnal but mighty to the pulling down of strongholds. (2 Corinthians 10:4-5)

- In Jesus' Name, I ask Abba Father to remove every veil from my eyes, soul, and spirit so I may receive everything God has for me.
- I ask Abba Father to destroy any remaining logic systems, schematics or personal or ancestral patterns of iniquity bringing bondage to my life.
- With the help of Holy Spirit, I confess all personal and ancestral iniquities relating to bondage and/or addiction, including _____.
- I choose to forgive those who tempted me or hurt me through addictive behaviors or codependency.
- I pray this all in the Name of the Lord Jesus Christ Who will strengthen me and protect me from the evil one. (2 Thessalonians 3:3)

You have now bound the strongman of bondage and addiction!

Sketch by Barbara De Simon; Creative
Director of ROOTED Publishing.

**Look through this list and check each indicator that
is true of you and/or your direct line of ancestors:**

(Note: an * is used to designate where a definition is taken, at least in part, from online dictionaries.)

☐ Accusation. *(the accusing of somebody, or the state of having been accused of something wrong) (Revelation 12:10)

Addictions to:

    ☐ Alcohol.
    ☐ Caffeine.
    ☐ Cell phones.
    ☐ Cigarettes.
    ☐ Computers.
    ☐ Diet pills.
    ☐ The dominance of others. (unhealthy soul ties)
    ☐ Doubting salvation.
    ☐ Drugs. (legal or illegal)
    ☐ Food: anorexia, bulimia, etc.
    ☐ Hoarding. (excessive hanging on to things that you really don't need and may never use, especially when out of fear of being in lack)
    ☐ Medications (above and beyond prescribed use).
    ☐ Nicotine.
    ☐ Sex. (insatiable desire for sex) (Ezekiel 16:28-29)
    ☐ Sugar.
    ☐ Television.
    ☐ Video games.
    ☐ Work.
    ☐ Other_____.

☐ Anguish of spirit. *(extreme anxiety or emotional torment) (Romans 2:9)

- ☐ Anxiety. (1 Peter 5:7; Philippians 4:6-7)
- ☐ Bitter. *(angry and resentful) (James 3:14; Deut. 28:30; 1 Samuel 5:6; Job 7:11; Proverbs 18:19; Ephesians 4:31)
- ☐ Bound. (restricted, limited, not free in the Spirit)
- ☐ Brokenhearted. (Figuratively, having your heart fragmented to pieces,) (Psalm 51:17)
- ☐ Bruised spirit. *(hurt and upset, especially as a result of something that has damaged your self-esteem) (Ezekiel 23:3)
- ☐ Compulsive behavior. *(driven by an irresistible inner force to do something) (Proverbs 5:22; John 8:34)
- ☐ Compulsory subjection & control. *(forced, caused by force, or using force to make somebody do something)
- ☐ Codependency. *(a situation where a person, such as the partner of an alcoholic or a parent of a drug-addicted child, needs to feel needed by the other person)
- ☐ Condemnation. (feeling condemned even when forgiven) (2 Corinthians 3:9; Romans 8:1)
- ☐ Control.
- ☐ Coveting wealth in order to hoard it. (Luke 12:16-21)
- ☐ Criticism or critical spirit. (1 Peter 2:1)
- ☐ Death wish. (Isaiah 8:19)
- ☐ Dominance. *(power exerted over others - control or command wielded over self or others)
- ☐ Dominated by others. (soul ties)
- ☐ Doubting salvation. (2 Corinthians 13:5)
- ☐ Driven. *(striving to achieve personal goals because of a strong need or inner compulsion)
- ☐ Embarrassment. *(acute self-consciousness - a feeling of painful self-consciousness, uncomfortableness, shame, or humiliation) (Ezra 9:6)

False:

- ☐ Burden. *(burden, worrying responsibility, difficult or worrying responsibility or duty)

- ☐ Compassion.
- ☐ Guilt.
- ☐ Humility. (Galatians 6:3)
- ☐ Responsibility.
- ☐ Fault-finding.
- ☐ Fear of death. (Hebrews 2:14-15)
- ☐ Other fears. (Romans 8:15)
- ☐ Feeling "lost." (Hebrews 2:3)
- ☐ Frustration. *(a feeling of disappointment, exasperation, or weariness caused by goals being thwarted or desires unsatisfied)
- ☐ Gluttony. *(the act or practice of eating and drinking to excess) (Romans 16:18; Philippians 3:19)
- ☐ Gossip. *(habitual talker, somebody who habitually discusses the personal details of others' lives) (2 Timothy 2:16; Proverbs 20:19; 2 Corinthians 12:20)
- ☐ Hopelessness. *(despairing, feeling or showing no hope) (Proverbs 13:12)
- ☐ Hyperactivity. (might be linked to the spirit of necromancy) *(unusually active, restless, and lacking the ability to concentrate for any length of time, especially as a result of attention deficit disorder)
- ☐ Idleness. (inactive, not working, refusal to engage in beneficial activity) (Proverbs 19:15)
- ☐ Inability to break free. (Isaiah 58:6)
- ☐ Judging. (Isaiah 58:6, Romans 14:13)
- ☐ Maladies and forms of sickness that may be demonic in nature:
- ☐ ADD/ADHD. *(Attention Deficit Disorder/Attention Deficit Hyperactive Disorder)
- ☐ Chronic Fatigue Syndrome. *(an illness without a known cause that is characterized by long-term exhaustion, muscle weakness, depression, and sleep disturbances. It may be a reaction to a viral infection in somebody already debilitated) (demons can work symptoms just like CFS)

- [ ] Demon bites. (bites of unknown origin – usually infected and very slow healing)
- [ ] MPD/DID. (multiple personality disorder / dissociative identity disorder) (Please note; MPD/DID are not inherently demonic but may be used by demons to hold people in bondage.)
- [ ] Paranoia. *(1. Distrust: extreme and unreasonable suspicion of other people and their motives. 2. Psychiatric Disorder: a psychiatric disorder involving systematized delusion, usually of persecution) (Deuteronomy 28:67)
- [ ] Phantom pain. (felt pain without a cause – not due to loss of limb)
- [ ] Schizophrenia. *(A severe psychiatric disorder with symptoms of emotional instability, detachment from reality, and withdrawal into the self.) (Many times, fragmentation of soul can give access to demons that produce symptoms that are easily misdiagnosed as schizophrenia.) (Deuteronomy 28:28-29)

Deliverance ministers have different views on schizophrenia. Some think schizophrenia is completely demonic; others think it may be physical or mental in nature.

Schizophrenia is a reality, but at this point, I believe what is diagnosed as schizophrenia may be physical, and/or mental, and/or spiritual in nature. I also believe demons may be active in schizophrenic behavior regardless of its root cause.

Ida Mae Hammond shared the vision of the hand she received from God for ministering to schizophrenia in Chapter 21 of *Pigs in the Parlor*, Impact Books 2003, 2008.[2] John Eckhardt and the late Pat Legato both have excellent teachings on schizophrenia and fragmentation from a deliverance minister's viewpoint.

- [ ] Tourette's syndrome. (Tourette syndrome) is an inherited neuropsychiatric disorder with onset in childhood, characterized by multiple physical (motor) tics and at least one vocal (phonic) tic. These tics characteristically wax and wane, can be suppressed temporarily, and are preceded by a premonitory urge. Tourette's is defined as part of a spectrum of tic disorders . . .. Wikipedia Free Dictionary) (demonic activity may cause very similar symptoms)

☐ Manipulation. *(to control or influence somebody or something in an ingenious or devious way)

☐ Mind control. (Mind control, also known as brainwashing, coercive persuasion, thought control, or thought reform Wikipedia Free Dictionary.) (brainwashing by cultish, devilish or religious means) (controlling another's mind through manipulative or demonic means or through the hype, false prophecies, and the like) (Jeremiah 23:16, 25, 32)

☐ Nervousness. *(having a feeling of dread or apprehension) (Philippians 4:3-7, 1 Peter 5:7)

☐ Necromancy. *(The practice of attempting to communicate with the spirits of the dead in order to predict or influence the future.) (Signs of necromancy include the inability to shut the mind down, mind races or ringing in the ears.).

☐ No assurance of salvation.

☐ Obesity. (extremely overweight)

☐ Oppression. *(to subject a person or a people to a harsh or cruel form of domination) (especially when demonic or religious in nature) (Acts 10:32)

☐ Perfectionism. *(rigorous rejection of anything less than perfect)

☐ Possessiveness. *(wishing to control somebody exclusively or to be the sole object of somebody's love, tending not to share possessions with others) (Proverbs 22:7)

☐ Poverty. (the curse of mental poverty) (Deuteronomy 28:20-33, 38; Malachi 3:8-12; Psalm 34:9-10; Proverbs 6:9-11; 13:18) (The borrower is servant to the lender.)

☐ Continuing poverty may be linked to a spirit of mental poverty, especially when a poverty mentality continues regardless of the opportunity to earn a decent living.

- ☐ Pressure. *(constant state of worry and urgency, powerful and stressful demands on somebody's time, attention, and energy, or a demand of this sort)
- ☐ Rejection. (being or feeling cast off or discarded by others or God) (Judges 11:2-3)
- ☐ Resentment. *(ill-feeling, aggrieved feelings caused by a sense of having been badly treated) (Exodus 8:15)
- ☐ Restlessness. *(constantly moving, or unable to be still; seeking a change because of discontent) (Isaiah 28:12)
- ☐ Satanism. *(the worship of Satan, especially as a parody of Christian rites) (Acts 26:18)

Self:

- ☐ Accusation.
- ☐ Condemnation. (feeling condemned even when forgiven) (2 Corinthians 3:9; Romans 8:1; Job 9:20-21)
- ☐ Deception. *(the practice of deliberately making others believe things that are not true – or being deceived by the same) (Isaiah 8:19; 1 Timothy 6:5; Hebrews 3:12-13; Romans 1:30-31; Proverbs 28:18; Galatians 6:3)
- ☐ Destruction. (Leviticus 26:21-22; Job 26:6)
- ☐ Hatred. *(intense hostility, a feeling of intense hostility towards somebody or something) (Genesis 3; 7:3-4; 8; Deut. 28:22; Psalm 139:22; Proverbs 26:26; 1 Thess. 4:8)
- ☐ Indulgent. (tending to be tolerant and generally allowing yourself to have whatever you want, whenever you want)
- ☐ Pity.
- ☐ Reward. (overeating, etc.)
- ☐ Selfish ambition.
- ☐ Shame. *(a negative emotion that combines feelings of dishonor, unworthiness, and embarrassment) (Psalm 44:15; Revelation 3:18)
- ☐ Slavery. (Romans 6:15-16)

- [ ] Spiritual blindness. (2 Corinthians 4:3-4)
- [ ] Superiority. *(adopting or showing an attitude of condescension toward others)
- [ ] Uncontrolled spending.
- [ ] Unholy soul ties. (usually through fornication, unforgiveness, or putting others before God) (Matthew 5:27-28; Acts 5:1-4; Proverbs 22)
- [ ] Unrighteousness. (1 Peter 2:12)
- [ ] Unworthiness. *(feeling like you don't deserve anything or that you are lower than other's usual standards)
- [ ] Witchcraft. (using charms, potions or magical powers to manipulate others, etc.) (Nahum 3:4; Galatians 5:20)
- [ ] Worthlessness. *(having no good, attractive, or admirable qualities at all) (feeling useless or unsatisfactory) (Psalm 4:2)

Anyone having more than one or two of the previous indications of The Root Spirit of Bondage should pray the following in faith. The Bible says, "resist the devil and he will flee." The best way I know to resist the devil in prayers like this is to choose to cough, blow, or yawn by faith each time you see the word "Expel!" Resist the devil and he will flee! (James 4:7)

Pray and declare the following:

- In Jesus' Mighty Name I cast down spirits of:
- Accusation, Addictions, Anguish, and Anxiety. (Expel!)
- Bitterness, Codependency, Condemnation, and Controlling spirits. (Expel!)
- Gluttony, Gossip, and Hopelessness. (Expel!)
- Necromancy. (Expel!)
- Poverty, Rejection, and Slavery. (Expel!)
- In Jesus' Name, I bind and cast out The Strongman of Bondage. (Expel!)
- Heavenly Father I ask You to release freedom in me.
- I receive that freedom by faith just now.

ƛ I also ask You to release Your Spirit of Adoption to me.
ƛ I receive The Spirit of Adoption now, By faith in Jesus' Name.
ƛ Hallelujah, I am set free from bondage!
ƛ I give you praise. Amen.[3]

Deal with the head of the octopus-
The Root Spirit of Bondage:

ƛ In Jesus' Mighty Name, through His blood, and with the Sword of the Spirit I now cut off influence from The Head of Bondage.
ƛ I demolish the stronghold of bondage completely and thoroughly.
ƛ I bind The Strongman of bondage and impeach him from office in my life.
ƛ I resist The Root Spirit of Bondage and command it to release me and go NOW, in Jesus' Name. (Expel!)
ƛ In Jesus' Name, I forbid the head of the octopus, The Strongman of Bondage, and the stronghold of bondage to re-form, regenerate or in any other way reconnect to me or to the tentacles of the octopus that has operated in my life.

The Root Spirit of Bondage is now cast out and you are ready to move on.

Endnotes:

1   Dr. Douglas E. Carr, *Free Indeed from Root Spirits*. Create Space 2014.
2   Frank and Ida Mae Hammond, *Pigs in the Parlor*, Impact Books 2003, 2008.
3   Dr. Douglas E. Carr, *Free Indeed from Root Spirits*. From ministry prayer.

CHAPTER FOUR

THE TENTACLE OF REJECTION

Rejection is the devil's response to the Holy Spirit's conviction for one to forgive those who have hurt them. Forgiveness opens the door to deep healing of deep inner wounds. The opposite of rejection is the realization and acceptance of the truth God has never left or abandoned them. This brings people to a point of believing God can make everything work for the good to those who respond to His call, regardless of whatever trauma they have experienced.

I never understood how rejection worked against people struggling with addiction until Pam explained it to me. She shares her own story, and how God impacted her through teaching we received in an ISDM (International Society of Deliverance Ministers) in New Jersey:

I (Pam) will never forget when God opened my eyes regarding rejection. It was at an ISDM annual meeting in New Jersey.

Chris Hayward was explaining how we build up walls around our hearts to keep from getting hurt. Actually, there are several "walls of protection" keeping us from full surrender to God.

The first wall is the rejection of God. You may think you would never reject God, but I think we all have at some time or another. Have you ever wondered why circumstances turned out the way they did and why God didn't intervene? Is there some injustice you might perceive as God not answering your prayer? Perhaps an early death of a friend or a loved one. Maybe not getting a job you are qualified for. Perhaps you want a child and can't have a child. It could be any number of things that may make you feel like God doesn't love you. This is clearly a lie from the devil! Satan is the one who has been rejected by God, not you. John 3:16 comes to mind here. If God so loves the world, He so loves YOU.

The second wall is the rejection of self. Usually, we want what other people have. Perhaps you don't like the way you look. Or the talents God has blessed you with. Maybe you consider yourself a failure in life because of a mistake you have made that can't be changed. There are so many things Satan uses to lure us into the pit of depression.

The third wall is the fear of rejection. We build a wall because we are afraid of being rejected by others. Or by God! The fear of letting others know the real you, complete with all your mistakes and flaws, can be very real. What if who you are isn't good enough?

The fourth wall is the rejection of others. When this wall is in place, the fear of being rejected is so strong that you reject others before they can reject you. That leaves you alone and isolated. Satan loves that.

We all know Satan comes to steal, kill and destroy. He is a deceiver and a liar. He wants us to believe that we've messed up so bad God will reject us.

God wants us to succeed. He is on our side! We do have hope and a future. Satan is the one that has been rejected by God, not me, and not you!

Thanks, Pam for sharing your story! I (Doug) wrote on rejection in my book *Free Indeed! Deliverance Ministry*.[1] We also do a session on rejection in our MOD-2 *Breaking Free from Curses, Iniquities, and The Big Five Seminar*.[2]

I was surprised when the first tentacle I saw in the vision of the octopus of addiction was rejection. As I pondered on it and talked with Pam, it began to make sense. As Pam already mentioned, Satan is the one who was rejected. First known as Lucifer, he was among the chief angelic princes in heaven, but when he began speaking to his own heart that he would ascend to heaven and raise his throne above the stars of God, he ended up being kicked out of heaven. (see Isaiah 14:12-17 for example, that tells how the devil was cast down to the earth because of his prideful rebellion in the five times he decreed "I will," contrary to God's will) I discuss this more fully in my book *Choosing Kingdom*.[3]

Lucifer was renamed Satan, which means "accuser." Having been rejected because of his own proud and rebellious ways, he seeks to work rejection on humans in every devious way he can. He adds his thoughts, lies, and accusations to humans as whispers to their minds and souls - directed to change their perspective of things that happen.

He makes victims of sexual abuse feel it was their fault. He multiplies their pain by deceiving them into believing God either wasn't there when they were abused, or He didn't/doesn't care. Such lies build one upon another as walls around individual hearts.

People who feel rejected by their parents are attacked with thoughts they are unworthy of a parent's love, and if their own parent couldn't love them, no one else will be able to either. They usually end up hating and rejecting themselves too.

Rejection works in myriads of ways: fear of rejection, self-rejection, perceived rejection, feeling rejected by or rejecting others.

Ministry for Rejection:

꙳ Heavenly Father, I confess where I and my ancestors from the tenth generation have given in to rejection of God, self-rejection, fear of rejection, perceived rejection, and rejection of others.

꙳ I choose to forgive all those who have made me feel rejected or passed on to me an iniquitous pattern of receiving rejection or rejecting others.

꙳ Jesus was bruised for my iniquities!

꙳ By faith, I apply His blood to every iniquitous pattern of rejection in my life and ask You, God, to forgive me for walking in rejection.

꙳ Please cleanse me of iniquitous rejection and transform me through the blood of Jesus.

- I cancel every legal right rejection has had to work in my life and to tempt me to, or hold me in, the tentacle of rejection.
- I choose to resist demons working rejection in my life and cast them out through blowing or coughing in Jesus' Name and through His blood. (Expel by yawning, blowing or coughing!)
- I tear down walls of rejection including feeling rejected or rejection: God, myself, others, fear of rejection, perceived rejection and the like.
- I command every demon of rejection to leave now. (Expel!)
- I now chop the tentacle of rejection off twice and forbid it to regenerate, in Jesus' Name.
- Abba Father, I choose to receive Your love, acceptance, and forgiveness.
- In Jesus' powerful Name! Amen.

The tentacle of rejection is now cut off!

Sketch by Barbara De Simon; Creative Director of ROOTED Publishing.

DR. DOUGLAS E. CARR

Endnotes:

1   Dr. Douglas E. Carr, *Free Indeed! Deliverance Ministry,* First published by Esperanza Press in 2001. Later republished by Create Space in 2013.
2   Dr. Douglas E. Carr, Free Indeed Seminar, MOD-2 *Deliverance from Curses, Iniquities, and The Big Five!* Not yet published as a book, but currently available on CD and DVD from Doug Carr Freedom Ministries or Shekinah Church in Ann Arbor, Michigan.
3   Dr. Douglas E. Carr, *Choosing Kingdom,* Create Space 2017.

CHAPTER FIVE

THE TENTACLE OF INIQUITY

Any student of the Bible should understand how ancestral iniquity holds sway over four or more generations within a family line. The matter is confused, however, because many translations of the Bible translate the Hebrew words "Avon" and "Avah" as "sins," rather than their correct definition "iniquity."

Sin is usually defined as "missing the mark." It speaks of willful disobedience to God's known will. It may miss the mark by doing things people know God doesn't want them to do. That is committing "sins of commission." Or, it may miss it by not doing what they know God wants them to do. That is committing "sins of omission."

Iniquity, on the other hand, refers to a bent, twisting or distortion of character. I explain that more fully in the following quote I take from the first volume of *Getting to The Dirty Rotten Inner Core*.[1]

Iniquity (Avon): describes crookedness or perverseness; a moral distortion. It refers to the bent, perversity, twisting or pattern that affects generations of people and land. Iniquity describes character flaws behind the action of sin.

The word iniquity describes the character behind the action or sin. It is incorrect to use "sin" as a synonym of iniquity.

The Hebrew word is "Avon'" and is rightly translated iniquity 220 times in the King James Version. It is defined as:

1) Perversity, depravity, iniquity, guilt or punishment of iniquity
   1a) iniquity

1b) guilt of iniquity, guilt (as great), guilt (of condition)
1c) consequence of or punishment for iniquity.

"Avon'" comes from the word "Avah" that is translated: iniquity, perverse, perversely, perverted, amiss, turn, crooked, bowed down, troubled, wickedly, and wrong. Avah is defined as:

1) to bend, twist, distort
   1a) (Niphal) to be bent, be bowed down, be twisted, be perverted
   1b) (Piel) to twist, distort
   1c) (Hiphil) to do perversely
2) to commit iniquity, do wrong, pervert
   2a) (Qal) to do wrong, commit iniquity.

📖 But we are all as an unclean [thing], and all our righteousnesses [are] as filthy rags; (Used menstrual cloth – sign of infertility) and we all do fade as a leaf; and our iniquities, (Avon - bent, distortion, twisting or perversion) like the wind, have taken us away. And [there is] none that calleth upon thy name, that stirreth up himself to take hold of thee: for thou hast hid thy face from us, and hast consumed us, because of our iniquities. Isaiah 64:6-7 KJV.

Have you heard people say things like: "someone is a chip off the old block?" How about "like father, like son," "like the mother, like daughter" or "she/he is just like his father or mother?" Such things usually are true. When they are true in the negative sense, it is the work of generational iniquities as understood from the Hebrew words "Avon and Avah." (This brings a whole new meaning to "ding-dong –Avon calling!")

When you first visit a doctor's office, you are required to fill out your family history. Medical conditions in the family line set a pattern for the same or similar conditions in descendants.

The same is true concerning iniquity. It passes down ancestral lines. Thank God we can break iniquitous patterns! Jesus came to destroy every work of the devil! (1 John 3:8) He wants to break generational patterns of iniquities and the power of generational curses. He came for this very purpose and He will set us free IF we do it HIS way.

Something very familiar to "Avon and Avah" is seen in the New Testament. Consider the Greek word that is best translated "faults" but often mistranslated "sins."

"Faults" is defined as fall away, deviate from the right path, fall under judgment and come under condemnation. Strong's Concordance brings more light to the Greek word "faults" that comes from.

3895 parapipto (pronounced par-ap-ip'-to)
AV - fall away

1) to fall beside a person or thing,
2) to slip aside,
   2a) to deviate from the right path, turn aside, wander
   2b) to error
   2c) to fall away (from the true faith): from the worship
      of Jehovah

From root pipto:
AV - fall, fall down, light, fail.

1) to descend from a higher place to a lower
   1a) to fall (either from or upon)
      1a1) to be thrust down
   1b) metaphor-to fall under judgment, came under
      condemnation
2) to descend from an erect to a prostrate position
      2a1) to be prostrated, fall prostrate
      2a2) of those overcome by terror or astonishment or

grief or under the attack of an evil spirit or of falling dead suddenly

2a3) the dismemberment of a corpse by decay.

OK, I trust you have been patient with all this explanation. The Bible gives specific instructions on how to receive healing of generational curses and faults. However, many have missed something terribly important by a wrong translation of James 5:16. In my Bible program, six versions wrongly translate the Greek word (in italics) as I believe the NIV does.

  📖 Therefore confess your *sins* to each other and pray for each other so that you may be healed. The prayer of a righteous man is powerful and effective. (James 5:16, NIV)

The only version in my Bible program that translates the Greek word (in italics) correctly is the King James Version.

  📖 Confess [your] *faults* one to another, and pray one for another, that ye may be healed. The effectual fervent prayer of a righteous man availeth much. (James 5:16, KJV)

The Ten Commandments are given in Exodus 20:1-17. The concept of iniquity being passed down generationally is seen in verse five.

  📖 For I, the Lord your God, am a jealous God, visiting the iniquity of the fathers upon the children to the third and fourth generations of those who hate Me. (Exodus 20:5b, NKJV)

People are visited with the iniquities of their parents, grandparents, great-grandparents, and great-great-grandparents according to Exodus 20:5 and many other similar verses.

I do not fully understand it, but the same thing holds true concerning ancestral lines of adoptive parents, stepparents, and godparents. Iniquities are passed down through blood and/or legal means and people are under the sway of specific iniquities until a confession is made of personal *and* ancestral iniquity.

After thirty-plus years of jail ministry, I've witnessed this pattern countless times. When a person is in jail for addictive behavior I always ask, "do you have a parent or grandparent who is or was an addict?" The answer almost always is "yes." The same is true when I question people who are incarcerated because of criminal sexual behavior. They usually were either personally abused by a relative or have a direct ancestor who was a sexual predator.

Several years ago, I led a man to Christ who had been a heavy drinker, smoker, fornicator and had used a lot of chewing tobacco and snuff. He was also extremely overweight when I first met him. A few years later, this man discovered he had a son he did not know about. Twenty-some years previous, he had lived with a woman for a while, but they broke up and totally lost track of each other. As a young adult, this son decided to find his birth father. He was successful and I was privileged to witness them getting acquainted.

When I met this son, who had just learned his birth father's identity, it was incredulous! He was a spitting image of his birth father, only twenty-some years younger. Just like his father previously had been, the son was a heavy drinker, smoker, fornicator, and used chewing tobacco and snuff. He was also extremely overweight.

Isn't that amazing? This son was just like the father he had not previously met. He didn't pick up his father's previous behavior by example; it was part of his DNA. These iniquitous patterns were imprinted in him and flowed through his veins. I believe they were passed down spiritually through legal demonic assignments and physically through the blood.

In my book *From Woe Is Me to Wow Is He!*[2] I share how Jesus was bruised for our iniquities. He bled underneath (was bruised) the surface of his skin to provide a way for us to break the power of personal and ancestral iniquity by applying the blood from His bruises, to cancel inherited iniquities - including addiction!

It is interesting how addiction may skip a generation. For example, a grandfather may be addicted to alcohol, yet alcohol addiction passes by the son but enslaves a grandchild. The form of addiction may also change. The child of an alcoholic may be addicted to drugs. There are times when a child or grandchild gets saved and overcomes addiction to alcohol or drugs but becomes addicted to religion. I've heard people say, "Jesus is my high," or "I'm addicted to going to church and reading the Bible." Going to church and reading the Bible is great, but doing so out of addictive compulsion isn't nearly as good as doing so out of loving obedience and desire to commune with God.

The Bible instructs people to confess both personal and generational iniquities. This concept is expressed in Leviticus 26:39; Nehemiah 9:2; Ezra 9:7; Isaiah 65:7; Jeremiah 11:10, Lamentations 5:7, and perhaps the best known, from Daniel 9:6. I share two of these passages below.

📖 and they stood and *confessed their sins and the iniquities of their fathers.* (Nehemiah 9:2b, NKJV, emphasis mine)

📖 "O Lord, according to all Your righteousness, I pray, let Your anger and Your fury be turned away from Your city Jerusalem, Your holy mountain; because for our sins, and *for the iniquities of our fathers,* Jerusalem and Your people are a reproach to all those around us. (Daniel 9:6, NKJV, emphasis mine)

When we minister deep inner healing, we ask people to confess the iniquities of their ancestors on their mother's side and their father's side. They do not ask forgiveness for their ancestor's iniquity; they merely confess it. I take notes of the specific iniquities they confess, and we break each iniquitous hold off the person after they make a confession. If they have adoptive parents, stepparents, or god-parents, we have them include their iniquities as well.

The blood from Jesus' bruises not only has the power to break ancestral assignments and curses of iniquity, but it also makes provision for the corresponding blessing of what I call divine blood transfusion.

The Greek uses the interesting word *'sperma'* from which we get the English word *'sperm.'* I italicize the translation from *'sperma'* in two very familiar passages below.

📖 having been born again, not of corruptible *seed* but incorruptible, through the word of God which lives and abides forever, (1 Peter 1:23, NKJV, emphasis mine)

📖 Whoever has been born of God does not sin, for His *seed* remains in him; and he cannot sin, because he has been born of God. 1 John 3:9 NKJV. (emphasis mine)

There is a great power, IF and WHEN applied, in the seed (sperma) of God that becomes an active part in our regeneration when we are born again!

📖 For the word of God is living and powerful, and sharper than any two-edged sword, piercing even to the division of soul and spirit, and of joints and marrow, and is a discerner of the thoughts and intents of the heart. (Hebrews 4:12, NKJV)

Blood is somehow manufactured in our bone marrow. I don't begin to understand how this works, but I do know healthy blood is necessary in order to enjoy a healthy life.

It is important to understand; we can be born with unhealthy blood physically *and* spiritually. We inherit blood-borne diseases and predisposition to health problems. We also inherit blood-borne spiritual disease (I like to say "dis–ease," because a disease may include anything that steals our "ease.") We inherit a predisposition to continue in ancestral bents, distortions, or twisting of character. For the addict, this includes a bent toward addictive behavior that may be specific (i.e. alcohol, food, tobacco, etc.), or general (i.e. bent or twisting to addictive patterns and/or the weak victim or strong rescuer mindset of codependency).

To effectively break the hold of iniquity several steps are required: 1) Confession of personal *and* ancestral iniquity to God, 2) Applying the blood of Jesus' bruises to cleanse the blood of iniquity. 3) Forgiving those who brought specific iniquity into your family line. 4) Remitting sin and iniquity. 5) Confessing your faults to someone you can trust (in such a way your secrecy can be broken and accountability can be established. Once this is done, 6) The tentacle of iniquity can be cut off. We will do that one step at a time.

1) Confessing Personal and Ancestral Iniquity.

Holy Spirit is fully God. He knows everything about our ancestral lines. He will help us confess things we are not even aware of until we pray with his help. It helps to take notes while praying, recording each specific iniquity that comes to mind. Begin with confessing personal iniquities. Then move on and confess the iniquities of your birth father and his direct family line: both parents, and your grandparents, great grandparents, and great-great-grandparents on your father's and mother's side. Sin is only the expression iniquity. Our confession needs to speak to the underlying iniquity.

Be as thorough as possible in confessing the dirty rotten inner core or bent, twisted and/or distorted character in the family line.

Begin by praying "I confess my personal iniquities including. . .." Then do the same with the iniquities of your father and his family line, followed by the iniquities of your mother and her family line. If you have stepparents, god-parents, or adoptive parents do the same with their iniquities.

2) Apply the Blood from Jesus' Bruises to Break Iniquity and Release Cleansing.

📖 But He was wounded for our transgressions, *He was bruised for our iniquities*; The chastisement for our peace was upon Him, And by His stripes we are healed. (Isaiah 53:5, NKJV, emphasis mine)

Jesus was bruised for our iniquities. He bled underneath His skin where no one can see, leaving bruises visible to the eye. He bled internally (bruising) so we can apply His blood to break the power and the curse of the iniquitous patterns confessed in the first step. Use the notes you recorded in the previous step and, in prayer, apply the blood from Jesus' bruises to each iniquity from your list. When you have finished that, break every curse caused by personal and generational iniquity.

3) Forgive Those Who Brought Iniquity into Your Family Line.

Choose to forgive every person, including yourself, who has tainted your human blood with iniquity. Forgiveness is a matter of the will and one must willfully forgive in order to receive the deep healing needed. Simply choose to forgive each person, (including yourself) who contributed iniquity to your blood and forgive them for the way their iniquity made you feel.

4) Remit Iniquity Through the Blood of Jesus.

📖 Then said Jesus to them again, Peace be unto you: as my Father hath sent me, even so send I you. And when he had said this, he breathed on them, and saith unto them, Receive ye the Holy Ghost: Whose soever sins ye remit, they are remitted unto them; and whose soever sins ye retain, they are retained. Whose soever sins ye remit, they are remitted unto them; and whose soever sins ye retain, they are retained. (John 20:21-23, KJV)

Many translations substitute the words "forgive" and "forgiven" for the better words "remit" and "remitted" used in the King James Version. This is a huge mistake. Forgiving has to do with a pardon. Remitting cancels the sin and breaks the hold of the sin, and Satan's power to hold it against a person.

Jesus was speaking to his disciples and those who would become his disciples after being baptized in His Holy Spirit. He delegated the authority to remit sins through the baptism of His Holy Spirit. This authority was not limited to Peter or the others standing there with him. It certainly is not limited to the Catholic pope or priests. He released this authority to **all** who are baptized in the Holy Spirit and walking in the spiritual authority they have from their seats in the heavenly realms in Christ Jesus.

📖 And He raised us up together with Him and made us sit down together [giving us joint seating with Him] in the heavenly sphere [by virtue of our being] in Christ Jesus (The Messiah, The Anointed One). (Ephesians 2:6, AMPC)

John 20:21-23, properly translated, shows we are sent in Jesus' Name with power to remit (cancel or refrain from exacting or inflicting a debt or punishment; synonyms: cancel, set aside, revoke, repeal, rescind, abrogate, suspend) confessed sin so the devil loses his authority to continue using past sins against ourselves or those we minister to. Let me give you an example of such a declarative prayer:

In the Name and through the blood of Jesus Christ, I remit the sin and iniquity of addiction to . . .. and break its power off from . . .. this very day! I bind addiction to . . .. and release . . .. from it today! In Jesus' Name, amen. (Amen means "So be it!")

You can do that for yourself if you are saved and walking in spiritual authority. If not, ask someone else to remit your sins.

This is really powerful, especially when done by someone who has overcome addiction.

5) Confess Your Faults To One Another.

📖 Confess your faults one to another, and pray one for another, that ye may be healed. The effectual fervent prayer of a righteous man availeth much. (James 5:16, KJV)

This is a key component of freedom from addiction. It isn't enough to just tell God. In his section on healing, James tells us to confess our *faults* to *one another*. Many Bible translations use the word "sins" here to translate the Greek word "parapipto." I explain this much more thoroughly in the first volume of *Getting to The Dirty Rotten Inner Core*.[3] "Faults" is defined as fall away, deviate from the right path, fall under judgment and come under condemnation.

The very best way I know to do this is to confess your faults to someone who has overcome a similar fault. For example, one addicted to drugs may confess to someone who has overcome drug addiction and then receive prayer from that person.

I revised some prayers from the book I mentioned earlier to aid in this important step.

Prayer of confession to break the power of addiction.

⟩ Heavenly Father, I confess to You and to those around me;
⟩ I and my ancestors have given way to addiction.
⟩ I have particularly struggled with addiction to . . ..
⟩ Today, I confess and renounce addiction in my life.
⟩ I ask You to demolish every stronghold of addiction and cast out every demon working addiction in my life.
⟩ I now commit to receiving prayer to be healed of addiction.
⟩ In Jesus' Powerful Name. Amen.

Receive prayers of healing from the righteous:

⸜ Today, as we pray for our Christian (brother or sister),
⸜ We watch ourselves, lest we also are tempted.
⸜ We have heard this prayer of confession.
⸜ In Jesus' Name, we remit every generational and personal iniquitous pattern of addiction to . . ..
⸜ We plead the blood of Jesus Christ to bring complete healing and restoration from addiction to . . ..
⸜ We ask you, Abba Father, to bring us into the full release from addiction, so we can seek comfort from You alone, through Your Holy Spirit.
⸜ In the Name of the One who can and will do it: Jesus Christ our Lord. Amen.

6) Chop the Tentacle of Iniquity Off and Forbid it To Regenerate.

⸜ In Jesus' powerful Name, I take the sword of the Spirit and chop the tentacle of iniquity off twice.
⸜ I forbid the tentacle of iniquity to ever regenerate, in Jesus' Name, amen!

The Tentacle of Iniquity is cut off!

Pam made an interesting note to herself at this point and wanted to pray more on it before writing anything more, but it was so good I share it here. She wrote, "I saw Satan jealous of us as being loved and accepted and forgiven by God. That is why he uses iniquity against us so much because he knows that iniquity is an easy way to set up an idol (including addiction) in our lives."

Sketch by Barbara De Simon; Creative
Director of ROOTED Publishing.

Endnotes:

1 Douglas E. Carr, *Getting to The Dirty Rotten Inner Core.* Create Space, 2014.
2 Douglas E. Carr, *From Woe Is Me to Wow Is HE!* Create Space, 2016.
3 Douglas E. Carr, *Getting to The Dirty Rotten Inner Core,* pages 20-23. Create Space, 2014.

CHAPTER SIX

THE TENTACLE OF REBELLION

The strong tentacle of rebellion holds many addicts in self-destructive behavior. When parents tell their children to quit sucking their thumbs or give up their pacifier or favorite blanket, something rises up in them to cling to whatever source of comfort their mom or dad wants them to release. This is rebellion, which acts out in attempts to get one's own way.

The Kingdom of God refers to the "King's Domain," which extends as far as people voluntarily submit to His rule. To make this really simple; to engage in any type of addictive behavior contrary to the will of God is rebellion.

I (Doug) remember how terribly embarrassed I was when the pastor of the church I began attending saw me smoking my pipe. My Mother and Father smoked cigarettes and I hated the smell they left, especially in our home's only bathroom. For that reason, I never smoked cigarettes but chose cigars and pipes instead. Being "caught" by my pastor bothered me so much I finally mentioned it to him. He wisely responded, "your smoking doesn't bother me, but when God tells you to stop, stop!" This happened before I was even saved; God was at work. One day I was driving down the road, savoring my bourbon flavored pipe tobacco. I sensed God telling me to stop and I immediately threw my pipe to the pavement. When I arrived home, I destroyed my entire collection of pipes, tobacco, humidor, and cigars. For me, had I continued smoking after God told me to stop, it would have been rebellion.

My pastor was wise, and I use his counsel with others who talk with me about addictions. If Jesus tells you to stop, then stop, or you will be in rebellion. He will give the grace to stop when He tells you to stop. Grace is the God-given desire and power to do His will.

I was truly favored by the Lord and only endured one strong temptation to smoke a cigar after that. That, interestingly enough, was several years later when I was near the end of my junior year at Spring Arbor College. I commuted 50 plus miles each day from Hillsdale and there was a little store about halfway home, which was the only business in the small village of Pulaski, Michigan. For some reason, I was contemplating grace and the thought popped into my mind, "it would be OK if I stopped and bought a King Edward Cigar."

I had a strong hankering for a cigar, even though I had not smoked anything for over four years. I walked up to the counter and was surprised to hear the words come out of my mouth "I want a Baby Ruth candy bar." The owner handed me a candy bar, I paid him and pondered what happened as I ate it on my drive home. Three months later I was asked to pastor my first church, the only church in Pulaski, where the 129 residents living there at the time all knew everyone's business. I don't know whether I was being tested by God that day or if Satan was tempting me. I do know I am glad I didn't give in then or since. Rebellion can be serious!

First Samuel 15 tells how King Saul was stripped of his kingship because of rebellion. Many translations wrongly quote verse 23 "For rebellion is *as* the sin of witchcraft (or divination)." In the better translations the word "as," if used, is italicized, indicating it was added in an attempt to make the verse easier to understand. I believe it is more accurate to leave the word "as" out of verse 23, as seen below.

📖 For rebellion *is* the sin of witchcraft, and to break the word of the Lord is iniquity and idolatry. (1 Samuel 15:23, Jubilee Bible 2000)

Rebellion IS witchcraft because it exposes one to demonic influence which must be resisted, or it will establish a stronghold. Simon-Peter could tell you about that. There was a time earlier in his life when Jesus said to Peter:

📖 "Get behind Me, Satan! You are a stumbling block to Me; for you are not setting your mind on God's interests, but man's." (Matthew 16:23, NKJV)

Peter often failed miserably until the strong arm of rebellion was broken off his life. He learned, the hard way, how Satan can morph like an octopus to work his way into unsuspecting people. Years later, a wiser and more mature Peter wrote,

📖 Be sober, be vigilant; because your adversary the devil walks about like a roaring lion, seeking whom he may devour. (1 Peter 5:8, NKJV)

Let me explain *why* rebellion is witchcraft. God places authority over people to guide and protect them. Paul addresses this in Romans 13:1-7, and actually calls those in authority "God's ministers to you for good." When we rebel against God-given authority, we actually rebel against God and circumvent the protection He offers. The devil, prowling around like a hungry lion, is quick to take advantage of our vulnerability. That makes rebellion witchcraft because it exposes the rebellious to unchecked attacks of the enemy.

The church used to put legalistic restraints on people, but went too far and forbade behaviors not condemned in the Scripture; such as hairstyle, women not wearing pants, not watching any movies, television, and even using medicine. Legalism is never good, but the pendulum has swung too far in the other direction. The Church has become lax on things like cohabitation, premarital sex, addictive behavior, perversion, and many other things. Legalists and religious people tend to hate the sin and the sinner. Liberals seem to love the sinner and their sin! The Bible shows us a better way!

Jesus loved sinners enough to free them from sin!

John the Baptist said, "Behold the Lamb of God who *takes away* the sin of the world." The Lamb of God doesn't overlook sin, ignore sin, or bless sin. At the same time, He has no desire to condemn sinners. He loves people enough to free them from sin! How can we say we love people if we wink at things the Bible says will keep them from entering the Kingdom of God? Things like fornication, lying, murder, perversity, etc. are included in Bible lists of people who will not inherit the Kingdom of God. (1 Corinthians 6:9-10, Galatians 5:19-21, Revelation 21:8 for example)

Other things like moderate drinking of alcohol or smoking are not nearly as clear, unless God speaks to one personally, as He did to me, and says "Stop!" It is important to remember, however, if someone in authority over you tells you to stop, then you resist God Himself if you do not stop. Romans 13:1-5 indicates that rebelling against governing authorities is rebellion against God. That may be why Psalm 32:9 warns us not to be like a horse or a mule that must be held in by bit or bridle.

The opposite of rebellion is full abandonment to God's will. For the addict, this first means discovering God's will. Whatever the addiction may be, it becomes rebellion if it is done contrary to God's will. The question which begs to be asked is "Jesus, do you want me to continue this or not?" If His answer is "no," would it not be rebellion to continue?"

I realize it is harder for some to break addictive behaviors than others. It is harder for a two-pack a day smoker to quit smoking after 30 years than it is for someone who occasionally smokes a cigar or pipe. Therefore, the goal of submission is to take one step at a time as God leads.

Pam adds much to this book because she writes from the perspective of one who was addicted for years. Consider her honest reminiscing of how she struggled with addiction after she was born again.

I (Pam) didn't see smoking as being rebellious toward God. But now I had become a Christian, I didn't want anyone to know that I smoked. I had mixed feelings about quitting. I knew I should because it's not healthy. I watched my father die from lung cancer caused by years of smoking. But I also really enjoyed smoking; it helped me to relax, so I would use it to take a break. The way I came into agreement with Satan was believing other people were judging me. I thought if they only knew the real me, they wouldn't like me. I could feel myself pulling away from others because I felt embarrassed and guilty. I managed to keep my secret for a long time. I didn't share that I needed help. In my own strength, I unsuccessfully tried to quit for other people and for wrong reasons. I started to blame others for my problem. I started judging other people for judging me. They weren't judging me; Satan was getting me alone and attacking continually. That isn't a good place to be! I was falling into his trap. I realized that I was a liar just like him and he was stealing several areas of my life. He was on his way to destroying me. But God! God never came out directly and said: "quit." He gave me a choice. He said, "If you don't quit now, you will die." I quit!

Thanks, Pam, for your honest sharing! Pam quit smoking over a quarter of a century ago but reminds us of how vulnerable people can be. God is so committed to helping vulnerable people find true freedom that He sent his son to shed his blood for our healing and freedom.

Jesus shed His blood in seven specific places, so we can apply it to break seven specific curses going all the way back to Adam and Eve.

In the first garden, Eden, Adam and Eve knew God's will included not eating from the tree of the knowledge of good and evil. Satan deceived Eve into eating of it, and once she fell into sin, she convinced Adam to eat some too. They both tried to cover themselves and hide from God. In His love, He called out to them "Where are you?" Certainly, our God who sees all, already knew where they were.

God wanted them to own up to their sin and confess it, but they chose to blame others rather than take responsibility. They received due recompense for their sin. Still, God so loved them so much He took the blood of innocent animals to make them garments of skin to cover their nakedness.

Do you think a person's greatest temptation comes from the devil or from their own will? Which was true of Jesus?

Jesus was tempted in every way such as we are, yet was without sin. I think His greatest season of temptation occurred in the Garden of Gethsemane, rather than the desert where the devil tempted Him. In the desert, Jesus wrestled against the devil. In Gethsemane, He wrestled against His own will and desire to self-protect. Jesus took His three best friends with Him to the garden and asked them to watch and pray. He went a stone's throw further and began praying with great agony. "Father, if it is possible, remove this cup from me." He prayed thus several times, and each time concluded His prayer with "Nonetheless, not My will but Yours be done."

Jesus walked back to His closest friends, only to find them sleeping. How disappointed and alone He must have felt. He woke them and went back and began to pray again. He was in such agony at this final point of surrender that Dr. Luke records,

📖 And being in an agony he prayed more earnestly: and *his sweat was as it were great drops of blood* falling down to the ground. (Luke 22:44 KJV, emphasis mine)

Jesus did not resist to the shedding of blood when He was tempted by the devil, but He did resist to the shedding of the blood over "Nevertheless, not My will but Yours be done."

In the first garden, Adam and Eve gave into temptation and lost the battle. In the second garden, Jesus overcame temptation, but the battle was so difficult his blood vessels broke near his sweat glands and he actually sweated drops of blood. (This actually happens to people under great stress and is medically called "hematidrosis," or "Hematohidrosis" and is also called "blood sweat.")

We can apply the blood Jesus sweat in the Garden of Gethsemane to break the curse of a selfish and self-protective will that seeks comfort outside the will of God. We can break the power of personal rebellion. We can invoke the blessing of total surrender and abandonment to the will of God by the same blood.

I have revised the prayer from chapter 2 of *From Woe is Me to Wow is He!*[1] to begin the prayer for this chapter.

Breaking the Curse and Invoking the Blessing:

- I declare I am redeemed by the blood of the Lamb out of the hand of the enemy!
- Heavenly Father, I invoke You, in the Name of Jesus, to hear and answer my prayer this day.
- Dear Jesus, thank You for resisting the temptation to think about Yourself or protect Yourself in the Garden of Gethsemane.
- Thank You for not throwing in the towel and falling asleep with Your best friends.
- Thank You for breaking the curse of selfishness, independence, and narcissism by saying "nevertheless not My will, but Yours, be done."
- Right now, Father, I ask You to take the blood Jesus sweat in the Garden of Gethsemane and break the curse of a selfish, self-protective, and rebellious will from my life.
- I invoke Your blessing of absolute abandonment to Abba Father's will.
- I invoke the blessing of your working in me both to will and to do Your perfect will.

- All to Jesus, I surrender, all to Him I freely give.
- Take my life and let it be, consecrated fully, Lord to Thee.
- Now, in the name and through the blood of Jesus, I command every demon that was empowered by this curse against my will, to let me go and leave me right now.
- I cast you out and command you to go to the feet of Jesus Now! (Expel!)
- Now in Jesus' Powerful Name I take the sword of the Spirit and chop off the tentacle of rebellion off twice and forbid it to ever regenerate.

The tentacle of rebellion is now cut off!

Sketch by Barbara De Simon; Creative Director of ROOTED Publishing.

Endnote:

1 Douglas E. Carr, *From Woe Is Me to Wow is HE!* Create Space, 2016.

CHAPTER SEVEN

THE TENTACLE OF PYTHON

Demons of python and sorcery feverously work together to hold people in chains of addiction. Python often manifests by choking an addict's throat and making it difficult or nearly impossible to resist demons by coughing, blowing or yawning in faith. Python squeezes the life out of people who struggle with addiction. He occasionally manifests by intense pressure on the chest that may be mistaken to be a heart attack.

Even though God quickly delivered me from addiction to alcohol and smoking, I was still a workaholic and addicted to a need to be needed. It took years to learn that my need to be needed was a love hunger, which led to hewing out broken cisterns that could hold no water. I finally understood when I realized how Jeremiah 2:13 applied to me personally.

📖 "For My people have committed two evils: They have forsaken Me, the fountain of living waters, *And* hewn themselves cisterns—broken cisterns that can hold no water. (Jeremiah 2:13, NKJV)

My broken cistern was thinking I could not survive without a woman in my life. I began dating my first wife when I was sixteen, married her when I was eighteen, and felt incomplete when she left eighteen years later. It took God Almighty to show me I needed to be complete and happy in him before I would have anything worthwhile to offer anyone who might become my wife.

When God began cleansing me so He could use me again,

I was horribly attacked by a python spirit. It happened on a Sunday morning after my alarm went off in time for me to get ready for church. I had horrible pain in my chest and could barely breathe. I felt like I had an elephant sitting on my chest. It was so hard for me to breathe I could scarcely voice a prayer. At first, I thought I was having a fatal heart attack.

I tried crying out to God, but words barely came out. I finally forced myself to shower and got ready to meet up with a friend to ride to church. I turned Petra on and played their song "We exalt thee" over and over. Python left as that song played.

As seen in the slave girl who earned a lot of money for her owner by fortune-telling, (Acts 16:16-24) python often works in partnership with sorcery. The English word "sorcery" is translated from the Greek word "pharmakeia," which is the root of the English word "Pharmacy," which certainly includes addictive chemical substances. Especially hallucinogens.

Malachi reveals an act of faith that meets a condition where God himself will rebuke the Devourer.

📖 "Will a man rob God? Yet you have robbed Me! But you say, *'In what way have we robbed You?' In tithes and offerings. You are cursed with a curse, For you have robbed Me,* Even this whole nation. Bring all the tithes into the storehouse, That there may be food in My house, And try Me now in this," Says the Lord of hosts, "If I will not open for you the windows of heaven And pour out for you such blessing That there will not be room enough to receive it. *"And I will rebuke the devourer for your sakes,* So that he will not destroy the fruit of your ground, Nor shall the vine fail to bear fruit for you in the field," Says the Lord of hosts; (Malachi 3:8-1,1 NKJV emphasis mine)

Addictions are tools of the Devourer. They devour a person's finance, health, relationships, and willpower. When people give a tithe (10%of their income) to the Lord's work, the

Bible promises God will rebuke the Devourer! Addicts must learn the power of tithing to bring Jehovah's rebuke to spirits like python.

The flesh, with Satan's help, resists the idea of tithing. People think they can't afford to tithe, or the church is just after their money. Nothing could be further from the truth. Addicts usually waste more money on destructive addictions than their tithe would add up to.

Either God or Satan gets every person's tithe. God receives it, or Satan devours it! When people voluntarily give their tithe to God, He blesses the remaining 90% of their income. He does through many means: blessing people financially, physically, spiritually and so on. When people withhold their tithe, the Devourer has the legal right to take more than 10% through addictions, health problems, tickets, accidents, bad investments and so on.

I learned this the hard way. I received divine protection from 1972–1987 when I faithfully tithed. That protection was taken from me when I quit tithing for a few years after I left the ministry for five years. I was angry with my ex-wife, the people of the church I resigned, and with God whom I blamed for allowing me the pain of divorce and quitting the ministry.

With God's protective barrier removed, the Devourer took full advantage of my disobedience. I had so many illnesses, accidents, traffic tickets, and wrong relationships that money slipped through my hands like water through a sieve. My expenses soared including medical, insurance, phone, repair bills and the like. I am happy to report everything reversed for me when I again began honoring God with my full tithe each week.

I learned the hard way: people cannot afford to not tithe! This seems doubly true of addicts. Python enters disobedience concerning the tithe and robs the addict many-fold what their tithe would be through expensive addictions that devour their money.

God uses tithing to bless the obedient.

God rebukes the devourer when we tithe. He opens the heavens and pours out blessings including self-control, victory, and an overcoming mantle to rise above anything designed to hold one in patterns of addiction.

**Satan uses disobedience concerning the tithe
For permission to devour, kill, steal and destroy.**

I sense the tentacle of python cannot be cut off until a person comes into obedience concerning the tithe. Therefore, I encourage the reader to settle the Lordship question concerning tithe before praying the following prayer.

Ministry to break bonds of python.

- Heavenly Father, in Jesus' Name I confess where I and my ancestors to the tenth generation have withheld our tithes from You.
- I realize You are just in handing me over to the devourer because of my disobedience.
- I ask You to forgive me and break python's grip over me and my finances.
- Today I repent of not tithing and commit to bringing the full tithe into the storehouse (church offering) every week.
- I ask You to break the curse I and my ancestors have brought upon me and my descendants by not tithing.
- In Jesus' Name, I bind the strongman python and demolish its stronghold.
- In the name and through the blood of Jesus I rebuke and expel every demon that has taken advantage of my disobedience concerning God's word about tithing in Malachi 3:8-11. (Expel!)

- Strongman Python, I command you to let go of me, come out, and leave me right now, in Jesus' Name, amen. (Expel!)
- In Jesus' Name, I ask You, Heavenly Father, to break the hold and assignment of the devourer off from me and my descendants as we come into alignment and bring our full tithe into Your storehouse. (Expel!)
- Now, in the matchless Name of Jesus, I chop the tentacle of python off twice and forbid it to regenerate.
- Lord, I ask You to restore to me all the enemy has stolen. In Jesus' Name, Amen.

The tentacle of Python is now cut off!

Sketch by Barbara De Simon; Creative Director of ROOTED Publishing.

Endnote:

1   Dr. Douglas E. Carr, *From Woe is Me to Wow is He!* Create Space, 2016.

CHAPTER EIGHT

THE TENTACLE OF FRAGMENTATION

Many addicts feel "alas, two souls within my breast abide." They seldom understand their personal fragmentation which was probably caused by trauma earlier in their lives. This may become a full-blown dissociative identity disorder, often referred to as D.I.D.

I believe we all experience some mild dissociation. When one's mind wanders while listening to a friend, spouse, or sermon we experience mild dissociation. In a very real way, we temporarily go "somewhere else" in our thoughts and temporarily forget where we are and what we are doing.

I once got caught up in thinking about a jail service while driving 45-minutes home from preaching in a county jail. I had both hands on the wheel and thought I was paying attention, but suddenly didn't know where I was. I looked at street signs but didn't recognize any of the roads for several miles. Finally, I saw a familiar road and realized I had driven all the way through a small town with two stoplights and didn't even realize it. I wondered if I had been asleep at the wheel. It scared me so much I began asking people to accompany to and from jail services for a while.

I don't think I fell asleep that night while driving, I think I was so caught up in what happened earlier that I wasn't mindful of the present. What I experienced was mild compared to the dissociation identity disorder many people, including many addicts, live day in and day out.

James speaks of double-minded people. He may have been addressing people who were not sure whether to risk being shunned from family members if they converted from Judaism to Christianity. At the same time, what James describes is very similar to dissociative identity disorder and bears consideration.

It helps to look at the compound word James coined "double-minded." Bible scholars believe James invented this phrase because it is first mentioned in early literature the two times it is found in the Book of James. In the Greek "double-minded" is a compound word made up of "di" which can mean "divided" or "two," and "psuchos" which is translated as "soul" or "life." A literal translation can be "two – souled," or "divided soul."

📖 Such a person is double-minded and unstable in all they do. (James 1:8, NIV)

The Amplified Classic Bible takes the liberty of translating "psuchos" as "minds."

📖 [For being as he is] a man of two minds (hesitating, dubious, irresolute), [he is] unstable *and* unreliable *and* uncertain about everything [he thinks, feels, decides]. (James 1:8, AMPC)

So, what does it mean to be double-minded? (James 1:8; 4:8) The term "double-minded" comes from the Greek word "di-psuchos," meaning "a person with two minds or souls."

James writes of the doubting person, "he is "like a wave of the sea, blown and tossed by the wind. That man should not think he will receive anything from the Lord; he is a double-minded man, unstable in all he does." (from James 1:6–8)

People who have a love/hate relationship with themselves, or with others, may be double-minded. Jesus spoke of double-mindedness when He said no man can serve two masters because it creates a love/hate relationship within a person.

Such a person's greatest battles are within. One torn by such inner conflict can never fully lean with confidence in God and His gracious promises.

Double-minded people are "unstable in all their ways." They want to love their children and spouses but find themselves being cruel, mean, selfish, or neglectful. They want to serve Jesus - they truly WANT to love God and feel His love – but as much as they strive there is part of them that cannot believe God's love. This is more than "having one foot in Christ, and the other in the world!"

Many addicts truly love Jesus and want to serve him. I think it is unfair to tell them "If you just loved Jesus more you would overcome your addiction." Some addicts can quote Scriptures and have studied the Word of God. A huge part of them wants to walk in freedom, but there are other parts that lack the strength to do what the Bible tells them to do. That is exactly how fragmentation and/or D.I.D. works.

It is important for addicts, and those who work with them, to understand how Satan uses fragmentation, (also known as dissociative identity disorder) to manipulate people who want to serve Jesus but repetitively fall back into addictive behaviors.

Recently the Lord showed me how spirits of religion can "help" fragmented Christians memorize Scriptures, even like Satan (the reject from heaven) did when he used Bible verses against Jesus. Spirits of religion actually move addicts into a form of religion that denies the power they need to stay free. This causes an incongruence that calls for greater grace in ministering to addicts.

Satan knew the Bible well enough to quote it to Jesus. He could quote the words verbatim, but as James says, those who know the Word but do not live it out have only deceived themselves. (loosely paraphrased from the passage below)

📖 Therefore lay aside all filthiness and overflow of wickedness, and receive with meekness the implanted word, which is able to save your souls. But be doers of the word, and not hearers only, deceiving yourselves. For if anyone is a hearer of the word and not a doer, he is like a man observing his natural face in a mirror; for he observes himself, goes away, and immediately forgets what kind of man he was. But he who looks into the perfect law of liberty and continues *in it*, and is not a forgetful hearer but a doer of the work, this one will be blessed in what he does. (James 1:21-25, NKJV)

Many "on-again, off-again" people who vacillate from victorious faith to hopeless addiction suffer fragmentation from the trauma they experienced in childhood, youth and beyond. They may be able to quote Scripture wonderfully, and I believe it is engrafted to parts of their souls, but they have other fragmented parts of themselves that remain rebellious against God.

Satan could quote Scripture also, but he too is broken by his expulsion from heaven caused by his own rebellion and pride. Though he knew some Bible verses, the Bible was not engrafted into his soul. Therefore, he knew the Word but lacked the power to flesh out the truth of Scripture into humble service to Jehovah. He got kicked out of heaven and ended up using the Scriptures as weapons to attack Jesus, the righteousness of God!

People find freedom when each part of them personally knows both the Word of God *and* the God of the Word.

The kicker is: they need may need healing
of fragmentation before they can know God
in every part of their troubled souls!

Some people need help in becoming whole *before* the Bible becomes for them the truth Jesus said will set people free. John the Baptist did say "Behold the Lamb of God who **takes away** the sin of the world!" At the same time, when a person is fragmented, part of the person can receive what the Lamb of God offers, while another part of them continues to rebel against God.

I have worked with many who fully overcame addition while incarcerated in jail or prison. I've known others who have found ways to continue in addictive behaviors while serving time. I've been told it is far easier to tap into supplies of drugs while locked up than we might imagine. Surprisingly, some who continued using while incarcerated sounded really spiritual and had great head knowledge of Scripture. This well illustrates who dissociative identity disorder works.

Many addicts face a greater threat from other addicts in prison than from evil companions on the outside. We will discuss imprinting in Chapter 10, but we must understand: people struggling with fragmentation usually have good and evil companions (alters) living *inside* them. (An alter is a distinct personality or identity broken off a person's core.)

Let me explain. When people endure trauma or victimization beyond their coping skill or maturity level, fragments of their inner core may break off and create a condition called dissociative identity disorder. This often begins in childhood with those who suffer great trauma, abuse, abandonment, rejection or the like. For some, fragmentation began while they were still in the womb. This is most common in those conceived out of wedlock or those whose parents were addicts and/or given to violence.

Dissociative identity disorder is far more common than people might imagine. Addicts often have fragmented alters who hold on to addictions even when their core personality chooses to overcome addiction. This is very similar to how James describes double-minded people. Not all double-mindedness comes from fragmentation, but I believe much of it does. Likewise, not all fragmentation is double-mindedness, but enough of it is that we should take a deeper look at it here.

I take the following from my book, *Abundant Living as a Lifestyle rather than an Event*, published in July 2019.

I challenge your thinking as we enter this chapter. Do you think double-mindedness is a choice or a condition? Does an adult who was neglected, abused, molested or sodomized choose to be fragmented and/or double-minded, or has the trauma they experienced caused a condition they never would have chosen? There are no easy answers to that question, so I challenge you to consider possible etymologies of doublemindedness.[1]

Double mindedness can be a protective condition/ gift from God.

James coined the phrase "double-minded." In the Greek, it is a compound word made up of "di" and "psuchos" and is literally translated "two–souled." Its meaning is very similar to the term "broken-hearted."

Double-mindedness often comes through a trauma that is so painful a person becomes "broken-hearted." Part of their soul breaks off from their core. This is common when young people are abused or adults are so traumatized, they cannot handle it at the time. I believe this can be a gift from God. I think of a woman whose father began sexually abusing her when she was an infant. A baby can't handle such great trauma, so God, in His grace, allowed a specific part of her to separate until the time came where she was mature enough to deal with the pain.

Part of Jesus' mission was to bind up the wounds of the broken to shivers hearted (Luke 4:18 as quoted from Isaiah 61:1). We are sent to go and do likewise! People who were fragmented through trauma did not choose to be traumatized and they do not choose to be unstable in any of their ways.

The cure for fragmentation is deep healing and deliverance.

Deep Healing, deliverance and discipleship should all be part of helping people overcome addictive behaviors.

Double-mindedness can come when wavering between two decisions. I use the illustration of traditional Jews who became convinced Jesus is the Messiah when He walked their streets before He was hung on a cross, died, was buried and rose from the dead. I then compare their situation to that of modern-day people who are trying to decide whether they will follow Jesus all the way or hang on to some of their own lifestyles.

You hear of signs, wonders, and miracles among those who follow the resurrected and ascended Christ. You become convinced they are right. Jesus is indeed the Messiah! That makes you halt between two opinions. You can continue going to Synagogue, following the old methods of religion and worship, or you can openly acknowledge Jesus is the Anointed One. You can keep your new faith secret, or publicly confess Jesus as Lord and choose to seek first the Kingdom of God and His righteousness. Of course, if you do that, it might cost you everything that is familiar to you. This dilemma of fence-riding was a common struggle for new Jewish believers back then. Is it not still true of anyone who has to decide whether to break free from the Kingdom of Darkness to seek first the Kingdom of God and his righteousness?[2]

The cure for indecisiveness is
committing to follow Jesus as Lord.

Considering the things discussed in this chapter, it is easy to see how complex and difficult ministry might be for those hoping to overcome addiction. Deep healing from trauma, including trauma while in the womb, is often needed to set captives free. Even after a captive is set free, close personal discipleship is necessary to help people maintain personal freedom. Such ministry requires great love, commitment, and dedication from both the one ministering and the one being ministered to. When

Dr. Douglas E. Carr

two such people join in the work with the help of the Holy Spirit, they become a threefold cord that is not easily broken!

Ministry to break the hold of fragmentation.

ꝼ Heavenly Father, Luke 4:18 tells me Jesus came to bind up the wounds of my broken heart.

ꝼ Jesus wants to heal my broken heart and break the hold of fragmentation in my life.

ꝼ Today I choose to forgive the specific individuals who brought fragmentation and broken-heartedness into my life.

ꝼ I choose to forgive . . .. for . . ..

ꝼ Lord Jesus, now that I have forgiven those who hurt me the most, I ask You to remove every foothold the devil has had through my lack of forgiveness.

ꝼ I ask You to now rebuke the tormenter and I choose to expel it by coughing and/or yawning. (Expel!)

ꝼ Jesus, Your own heart was broken and fragmented when You took our sins upon Yourself when You hung on the cross.

ꝼ Your heart broke when You experienced God forsaking You when You, The Lamb of God, was sacrificed for my sin and the sin of the world.

ꝼ When a soldier pierced Your side with a spear, blood and water flowed out from Your own broken and ruptured heart.

ꝼ Today I apply Your blood and water to my broken and fragmented heart and receive Your healing by faith.

ꝼ I confess where my brokenness has held me in addictive behaviors.

ꝼ I also receive and declare Your healing of my broken heart which empowers me to rise above addiction to live in victory.

- In Jesus' Name, I chop the tentacle of fragmentation off with a double cut and forbid it to regenerate.
- Thank you, Jesus, for healing my broken heart and making me whole again. Amen.[3]

Sketch by Barbara De Simon; Creative Director of ROOTED Publishing.

Endnotes:

1   Dr. Douglas Carr, *Abundant Living as a Lifestyle Rather than an Event,* Kindle Direct Print, July 2019.
2   I have not been able to locate the source of this quote. I believe it came from an Internet commentary study on the book of James.
3   See Chapter 9: Taking back wholeness through His (broken) heart of *From Woe is Me to Wow is He!* for information about how to apply the blood and water from Jesus' broken heart to break the curse of broken-heartedness and invoke the blessing of wholeness. Doug Carr, Create Space, 2016.

CHAPTER NINE

THE TENTACLE OF TRAUMA

We discussed fragmentation in the previous chapter. Trauma often fragments people, leaving one part of them wanting to live the good life and other parts giving in to the throes of addiction.

My own brokenness as a teen and young man made me vulnerable to addiction. A teenager introduced me to pornography when I was too young to understand. Three others introduced me to fornication when I was in Junior High school. One of my best friends in High School introduced me to smoking and another one introduced me to drinking to excess.

I, like many who fall into addictive behavior, had enough personal hang-ups that I was willing to do just about anything to fit in with the crowd, even when my heart told me to resist. I'm sure every addict can relate.

While trauma doesn't force people into self-destructive behavior, it certainly paves the way for the destroyer to enter in.

Considering the trauma soldiers in combat face, is it any wonder so many now struggle with addictions? I remember a dear man who was traumatized by what he experienced in Vietnam. He was considered a helpless alcoholic by many, including his own wife and parents.

Without going into detail here, I note how many Vietnam veterans suffer from addiction. They were actually cursed by Buddhists as they entered Vietnam. Veterans of the Gulf War were cursed by Islamic priests (Inmans), many who cursed American soldiers five times a day during their prayer times.

I was called upon to minister to this alcoholic by his boss, who had come to know the love of God and the power of Jesus when I led him to the great salvation Jesus offers. As the man's boss, he was caught between two opinions. As the president of the company this man worked for, he knew he would have to fire the man if he continued to drink while driving the company vehicle. At the same time, he hated the thought of firing a man who was the sole provider for his wife and children.

The man's wife was hopeless when I first met them. She said, "There is no hope for my husband." She still loved him, but counseling, Alcoholics Anonymous, and other attempts at overcoming addictive behaviors had failed them completely – even though he did have a few short periods of victory.

Thankfully, the man turned to Jesus and was delivered totally from alcohol! The couple stayed married, had additional children, and enjoy a victory they deemed impossible until Jesus saved him from the gutter most to the uttermost.

Unfortunately, such testimonies are rare. Many addicts experience great trauma from their own inner wars. Salvation is a necessary entrance to the Kingdom of God but most people, especially traumatized addicts, need further care and ministry. To help veterans break such curses, we must lead them in forgiving their enemies before breaking the power of such curses through the blood of Jesus. Deep healing from trauma is often necessary before people are willing to forgive the enemy in order to break the power of curses. This sounds difficult, but Jesus wants to set every veteran free.

People are worth it! Jesus always started where people were and led them as far as they would follow Him into victory. We must do the same.

Jesus turned to a familiar Scripture from Isaiah 61 when He was inaugurated into his public ministry.

> "The Spirit of the Lord *is* upon Me,
> Because He has anointed Me
> To preach the gospel to *the* poor;

He has sent Me to heal the brokenhearted,
To proclaim liberty to *the* captives
And recovery of sight to *the* blind,
To set at liberty those who are oppressed. (Luke 4:18, NKJV)

God truly desires to set every captive free, and launch each one into their prophetic destiny! Admittedly, this freedom comes easier for some than for others, but the heart of Jesus still says to every seeker, "Neither do I condemn thee, go and sin no more." Jesus is familiar with suffering. He too was rejected, traumatized, forsaken and abandoned but He overcame and will help you and/or those you minister to overcome as well.

Ministry for overcoming trauma

- Lord Jesus, I have been through some things that really hurt when they happened. They still hurt to this day.
- Today I choose Your path of healing.
- I choose to forgive those who brought the greatest trauma into my life, including . . .. for . . ..
- I forgive them for what they did and for what they did not do.
- I also forgive them for how they made me feel, and how their actions changed the course of my life.
- I confess all the ways I have sinned against You and now receive Your forgiveness by faith.
- I also choose to forgive myself for everything you have forgiven me for.
- Jesus, I now gather all my trauma up and hand it to You.
- I trust You to remove everything from me I release to You!
- I receive Your healing touch to all mental, emotional, physical and spiritual scars this trauma has left.
- Now, in the mighty name of Jesus, I twice cut off the tentacle of trauma and forbid it to regenerate.

- I choose to yield my brokenness to You, trusting You to release healing and wholeness to me.
- Thank You, Lord, for Your healing and deliverance.
- Amen.
- Trauma: Be gone in Jesus' Name. (Expel!)

The tentacle of fragmentation is now cut off!

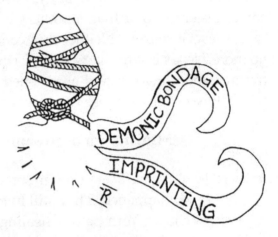

Sketch by Barbara De Simon; Creative Director of ROOTED Publishing.

CHAPTER TEN

THE TENTACLE OF IMPRINTING

Imprinting, in the technical sense, is any kind of phase-sensitive learning (learning occurring at a particular age or a particular life stage) that is rapid and apparently independent of the consequences of behavior.

When God gave me the vision of the octopus, however, and named one tentacle "imprinting," I knew He was referring to behavior learned from others, often accentuated by peer pressure.

I remember how my high school friend pressured me to start smoking so I could be cool. Even though I refused cigarettes for reasons mentioned earlier, I bought my first pipe and tobacco that very day from a store that didn't mind selling to minors. Groups of boys found places where they could smoke without being seen. They all puffed and exhaled in similar ways, and most smoked the same brand, but I was cool, puffing sweet-smelling tobacco from my pipe.

Television helps with imprinting. Before tobacco advertising was banned on television, we had the Marlboro Man. Who wouldn't want to be like him? Women were imprinted by the "You've come a long way, baby" of Virginia Slims. Imprinting, in this sense, may come from advertising, past or present family, friends, etc. For better or worse, we tend to unconsciously begin imitating those who have what we wish we could have.

I had the sad duty of preaching a funeral for an addict who had been an alcoholic until his friends introduced him to drugs. I liked the man and cared for him and his family, but had lost track of them. I had previously witnessed to him, but when I did, he said he believed in positive thinking, not God. I hope someone led him to salvation before he died. I know Jesus was a friend of drunkards and tax-collectors. I wished I had been a better friend.

This poor man died in a mobile home during really hot weather and wasn't found for several days. Of course, that meant he had to have a closed casket funeral. I was surprised at how many people showed up for his funeral. There were a lot of people who really liked him! I understood for he was a likable man, even though addiction got the best of him.

I agreed to do the funeral for two reasons. First of all, I cared for the family. But I also knew many of those who might attend his funeral would not have many other opportunities to hear the Gospel. Things went well until I mentioned the man had been an alcoholic until some friends introduced him to drugs. I made the mistake of speaking truth at the wrong time and place. I said, "True friends never introduce friends to drugs." When I said that, about a dozen people got up and walked out. I continued the message as asked, and, gave a chance to receive Jesus at the end, many raised their hands to receive Christ. I truly wished I would not have shared the comment that made several people walk out.

I believe imprinting is why many people begin addictive behavior. They do what their friends or heroes are doing. My friends and family led the way for me to become addicted. My dad used to say, "birds of a feather flock together." God says something very similar.

📖 Do not be so deceived and misled! Evil companionships (communion, associations) corrupt and deprave good manners and morals and character. (1 Corinthians 15:33, AMPC)

Thankfully, many are able to avoid the pitfall of drugs while locked up. Their minds become clearer when they are separated from their drug-using and drug dealers. Too often, however, many others turn back to addiction soon after they are released and return to previous places and companions.

Recently, while ministering at the jail, one inmate called out a verse and asked a chaplain to read it. Inmates can tell when other inmates are sincere, and this one was very sincere. He picked out a great verse, and the others paid attention. He shared why so many addicts quit while incarcerated, but fall back into addiction when they get out of jail. I share the verse he chose in two popular translations.

📖 Do not be deceived: "Bad company corrupts good morals." (1 Corinthians 15:33, MEV)

📖 Do not be deceived: "Evil company corrupts good habits." (1 Corinthians 15:33, NKJV)

Some of the most successful recovery programs remove recovering addicts from their neighborhoods and familiar friends. There is one program in our area that doesn't allow recovering addicts to use a phone, receive letters, or go out in public until they have proven themselves trustworthy of greater freedom. Some jails won't even accept letters for inmates in sealed envelopes because people have learned to lance the glue with drugs, showing how creative "bad company" can be in leading friends astray.

Unfortunately, many cannot afford the time off work required to take advantage of in-house recovery programs. Therefore, we need ways to help recovering addicts who have few viable options of where they can live or who they may run into.

One of my favorite stories as a child was *The Ugly Duckling*. It is a story by Danish poet and author Hans Christian Andersen (1805–1875). It tells of a homely little bird born in a barnyard who suffered abuse from the others around him until, much to his delight (and to the surprise of others), he matured into a beautiful swan. I loved the story because I felt like an ugly duckling for years. At the same time, I had something within my soul that made me think God had a plan for my life. I also needed affirmation to quit thinking I was an ugly duckling and begin believing God's destiny for my life.

Wikipedia summarizes the story better than I can.

> When the story begins, a mother duck's eggs hatch. One of the little birds is perceived by the other birds and animals on the farm as an ugly little creature and suffers much verbal and physical abuse from them. He wanders sadly from the barnyard and lives with wild ducks and geese until hunters slaughter the flocks. He finds a home with an old woman, but her cat and hen tease and taunt him mercilessly and once again he sets off alone.

> The duckling sees a flock of migrating wild swans. He is delighted and excited, but he cannot join them, for he is too young and cannot fly. Winter arrives. A farmer finds and carries the freezing little duckling home, but the foundling is frightened by the farmer's noisy children and flees the house. He spends a miserable winter alone in the outdoors, mostly hiding in a cave on the lake that partly freezes over. When spring arrives, a flock of swans descends on the lake.

> The ugly duckling, now having fully grown and matured, is unable to endure a life of solitude and hardship anymore and decides to throw himself at the flock of swans deciding that it is better to be killed by such beautiful birds than to live a life of ugliness and misery. He is shocked when the swans welcome and accept him, only

to realize by looking at his reflection in the water that he was in fact not a duckling, but a swan all this time. The flock takes to the air, and the now beautiful swan spreads his gorgeous large wings and takes flight with the rest of his new kind family.[1]

Jesus wants His church to love, accept and forgive people as He did. He wants Christians to exercise love and compassion toward addicts, rather than disgust and judgment on them. And Jesus demonstrated how loving acceptance is needed *before* addicts can conquer their addictions.

Jesus calls people out of their addictions *and* from their familiar friends so they can break the power of imprinting and become everything they were created to be.

The Chaplain and volunteers at the jail where I preach often remind the inmates, they need to choose new friends and not hang around with those they used to get drunk or high with. They need to CHOOSE whom they allow to imprint them!

Unfortunately, some churches aren't quick to welcome addicts. They think it is better to keep their people "safe" than to fulfill the great commission. But, even when churches fail, Christians can stand tall and befriend drunkards and addicts just like Jesus did!

Some Christians are so religious they hate the sin *and* the sinner. They don't want to be around people who are addicts or who have struggled with addictions. Thinking themselves to be religious, they prove themselves to be insensitive and uncaring for people who truly need their assistance.

Other so-called Christians go in the opposite direction. They love the sinner and the sin. They ignore what the Bible says about people who continue in sin. Rather than truly loving them and leading them to freedom, they let them die in their sin.

Jesus calls us to love the sinner enough to lead them to

freedom from their sin. He demonstrated how religious people condemned the woman caught in adultery (John 8). He also proved mercy is more redemptive than judgment by saying to the woman "Neither do I condemn you, go and sin no more."

Imprinting is negative when the devil is behind it. It is positive when the love of Father God, the compassion of Jesus, and the anointing of the Holy Spirit is behind it. My life has been greatly impacted by the imprinting of friends who love God, the Word of God, and the world Jesus died for.

Paul challenged the Corinthians by saying "Imitate me as I imitate Christ." Isn't that the highest form of imprinting, modeling the life of Jesus to others?

Ministry for overcoming imprinting

\ Father, I confess where I have allowed others to influence me to addictive behavior. (Confess every addictive behavior you began under the influence of specific people then forgive the people who influenced you to addiction)

\ I choose to forgive . . . for introducing me to . . ..

\ I confess I have been deceived and misled! I've allowed wrong friendships to influence me toward addiction.

\ I confess where I have wanted to "fit in" with people engaged in harmful activities . . ..

\ I now renounce harmful imprinting and wrong relationships that have held me in destructive behaviors.

\ I choose to step away from people who influence me to addictive behavior.

\ I choose to draw closer to those who will help me forever leave addictive behavior.

\ Now, in the mighty name of Jesus, I cut the tentacle imprinting off twice and forbid it to regenerate.

\ I choose to yield my relationships to You, trusting You to connect me to those who will help me find and keep my freedom.

- Thank You, Lord, for Your healing and deliverance.
- Amen.
- Imprinting, GO in Jesus' Name! (Expel!)

The tentacle of imprinting is now broken!

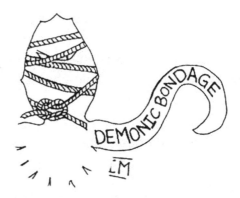

Sketch by Barbara De Simon; Creative
Director of ROOTED Publishing.

Endnote:

1   Wikipedia, the Free Encyclopedia: Plot of *The Ugly Duckling*.

CHAPTER ELEVEN

BREAKING FREE FROM SPIRITS OF ADDICTION

I believe the strongman over most addictions is The Root Spirit of Bondage. I have a whole chapter on that in my book *Free Indeed from Root Spirits.*

Even though I shared some of this at the beginning of this book, I want to share the first one and a half pages of that chapter below.

The Root Spirit of Bondage
(Addictive Behaviors.)

📖 For ye received not the spirit of bondage again unto fear; but ye received the spirit of adoption, whereby we cry, Abba, Father. (Romans 8:15, ASV)

📖 For freedom did Christ set us free: stand fast therefore, and be not entangled again in a yoke of bondage. (Galatians 5:1, ASV)

> The root of The Spirit of Bondage is the work of the flesh (Galatians 5:19-21). The fruit of The Spirit of Bondage is imprisonment to the devil, addictions, fear, and dishonesty.
>
> A few of the manifestations of this spirit are captivity to the devil, compulsive sin, bondage to sin and addictions, fear of death, and slave of corruption.
>
> There are various kinds of bondages. We usually think of things like addictions to alcohol,

anorexia, computers, playing video games 8-10 hours a day, workaholic, drugs or sex, etc. But codependency is also a strong delusion operating under The Spirit of Bondage.

With codependence, there are strong rescuers who "need" someone to rescue and weak victims who "need" someone to rescue them. They are convinced they can't live without the other. There are some cultures where the wife is burned to death on the husband's funeral pyre if he dies first!

Any behavior a person does not have mastery over may be evidence that The Spirit of Bondage is at work.[1]

Python is another strong demonic assignment holding people in addiction. Python often makes people feel like they are being choked around the neck or squeezed around the head, chest or stomach. When people sense that, we bind python and cast it out. I once had a lukewarm Christian walk into my office with her parents. She didn't believe Christians could have demons, yet she didn't make it two feet inside my office when she was thrown to the floor and began slithering across it like a snake. I cast the python spirit out and she stood up and was able to converse normally.

The Greek word, "pharmakeia" is translated "sorcery" in most English Bibles. It is the root of the English word "pharmacy." It represents the use of medicine, drugs or spells. Most secular treatment plans don't even consider how demons try to kill, steal and destroy the very addicts Jesus came to save.

Pharmakeia plays a huge part in drug addiction, including street drugs as well as the overuse of prescribed medications including opioids, pain killers, tranquilizers and the like.

A necessary first step to casting out demons is removing any legal rights the enemy has through unforgiveness, both of others and self. Jesus said unforgiving people are handed over to tormentors. Addictive behavior torments many. Paul shared how unforgiveness gives the devil one a legal area to stand in a person's life.

📖 "Be angry, and do not sin": do not let the sun go down on your wrath, nor give place to the devil. (Ephesians 4:26-27, NKJV)

Ministry for Overcoming the Stronghold of Addiction

⟨ God, I am ready to do whatever I need to do in order to overcome the strongman of addiction.
⟨ I know Jesus said if I don't forgive those who have hurt me, I will be handed over to the tormentor. (consider Matthew 18:21-35)
⟨ I am tired of being tormented!
⟨ Heavenly Father, today I make a bowl out of my hands, and place in that bowl each person who has brought torment into my life and/or contributed to my addictive behavior, including . . ..
⟨ (Place in the bowl what each person did, how it made you feel, and how they contributed to your addiction.)
⟨ I choose to forgive these people in Jesus' Name . . ..
⟨ I choose to hand this bowl of unforgiveness to Jesus now. (Try to visualize what He is doing with it.)
⟨ I also choose to forgive myself, Father, for the way I have failed you, myself and others through my addictive behaviors.
⟨ Now, in the mighty name of Jesus Christ and through His shed blood, I bind every strongman behind every addiction I've struggled with.
⟨ I demolish the stronghold of addiction, bringing it down with great spiritual violence, and impeaching the leader behind every demonic assignment of addiction.

- Now, in the name and authority of Jesus Christ and His shed blood, I command every other demon assigned to hold me in addiction to release me and leave me right now! (Expel by blowing or coughing in faith. Expect them to leave!)
- Now, in Jesus' Name, I cut the tentacle of addiction off twice and forbid it to regenerate.
- Heavenly Father, You are a good, good Father and Jesus promised You will give the Holy Spirit to those who ask.
- Right now, in Jesus' powerful name, I ask You to fill me with the Holy Spirit.
- Holy Spirit, I ask You to fill every area where demons worked addiction in my life.
- Please help me transition from shame to favor, and from condemnation to the conviction of the Holy Spirit.
- In Jesus' Name, amen!

The stronghold of addiction is now broken!

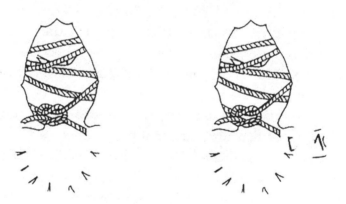

Endnotes:

1   Douglas Carr, *Free Indeed from Root Spirits.* Create Space 2014.

CHAPTER TWELVE

REPLACING THE STRONGMAN
WITH THE STRONG ONE!

Joshua told the people, "Choose this day whom you will serve." Jesus calls us to do the same. He said no one can serve two masters, because he will either love the one and hate the other or vice-versa. In context, he said, "You cannot serve both God and Mammon." You cannot serve Jesus and addiction either!

Addiction is a terrible taskmaster. It causes people to lose their health, self-respect, victory, and too often, family and friends. It often brings early death through health issues or fatal crashes while driving under the influence.

Mothers Against Drunk Driving (MADD) report, "Almost every day in America, another 30 people die as a result of drunk driving crashes. That's one person every 48 minutes." They also report, "57% of fatally injured drivers had alcohol and/or other drugs in their system – 17% had both."[1]

When addiction masters a person, it steals, kills and destroys the lives of addicts and innocent bystanders.

Jesus is a great master. If we faithfully walk with and follow him as Lord and Master, He will invite us to be his friends (John 15:14-15). He still calls people to deny themselves daily, take up their cross and actually follow Him. When they do, Jesus leads them to victory, abundant life on earth, and eternal life in heaven.

You have stripped the strongman of its arms! All that is left is the head that has lost its grip. You can now bind him, demolish his stronghold, and walk free of addiction!

Ministry to cast out the strongman of addiction.

⸸ Strongman of addiction, I bind you, break your power and demolish your stronghold in Jesus' Name.

⸸ I bring your stronghold down with great violence and impeach you from every hold you have had in my life.

⸸ I command you, strongman of addiction, to release me and leave me now in Jesus' Name and through His blood. (Expel!)

⸸ I forbid you to return to me.

⸸ I also forbid you to touch any of my family members.

⸸ I cover the tracks of what we have done here with the blood of Jesus.

⸸ I forbid any counter-attack or backtracking in Jesus' Name.

⸸ You are no longer my master. Your hold is broken completely in Jesus' Name, through His blood, and by His grace.

⸸ Root Spirit of Bondage, release me and go now! In the Name and through the blood of Christ Jesus the Lord!

⸸ Jesus Christ is my Lord, Savior, Healer, and Deliverer!

Everything you have done for yourself or helped someone else to do in order to be free and delivered has saved you or them *from* bondage. The enemy has been defeated but continues to war against the children of God until they fully manifest as mature disciples of Jesus Christ and sons and daughters of the Kingdom. The whole creation is waiting for this to happen, but until the return of Christ, it only happens one individual at a time.

Being *saved from* empowers us to be *saved to* Kingdom guidance and into being whom God created us to be, and doing what God prepared in advance for us to do. Therein life is more abundantly discovered.

When Jesus told His followers to seek first the Kingdom of God and His righteousness, He was speaking of a whole new kingdom. Rather than kingdoms of man or kingdom of self,

Jesus challenged us to turn from selfish repressive kingdoms of darkness to the Kingdom of Light.

Kingdom stands for "King's Domain." God is not a cruel dictator. His reign is not one of force, but one where He invites people to voluntarily submit to His rule one day at a time. He allows each individual to choose whom they will serve. Jesus said if we want to be His disciples, we need to deny ourselves, take up our crosses daily, and actually follow Him.

Prayer to make Jesus Lord of all.

⟍ Lord Jesus, I confess I have failed to follow You as Lord and Master.

⟍ I have allowed addictions to control me in the past, but today I repent and choose to turn completely from addiction.

⟍ You said if anyone wants to follow You, he or she must deny themselves daily, take up their cross, and follow You!

⟍ Today I choose to follow You.

⟍ I call upon You as Savior and choose to follow You as Lord of all.

⟍ You came to destroy the work of the devil!

⟍ I believe! Please destroy every work of Satan in my life!

⟍ I receive Your forgiveness, healing, and deliverance.

⟍ I choose to seek first Your Kingdom and Your righteousness today and each day hereafter.

⟍ In Jesus' Name, amen.

Endnote:

1   Taken from Mothers Against Drunk Driving (MADD) we Mothers Against Drunk Driving (MADD) website statistics.

ABOUT THE AUTHORS

Douglas Carr labored hard with limited results until he broke free from religious bondage and finally began letting Holy Spirit work in him and through him however he was prompted by God.

The Spirit-filled and Spirit-sensitive life has been and remains an ongoing challenge of 1) faith overcoming unbelief, and 2) the human spirit taking dominion over the soul and body in everyday life and ministry.

God has been good to Doug, blessing him with his wonderful wife, helpmate, and partner in ministry since 12-12-93. The very meaning of the numbers in the date God chose for their wedding was indicative of how they needed to grow together in the ways of Jesus Christ and His Holy Spirit.

Doug has ministered deliverance since the late 1990s. After a forty-day fast in 1999, he followed the Lord's prompting to attend Wagner Leadership Institute where he earned his Masters and Doctorate in Practical Ministry with concentrations in Deliverance and Intercession.

Dr. Carr sees the need to raise up ministers of deep healing and deliverance who walk in the fullness of the Spirit to bring healing and freedom to those so desperately need it.

During the Releasing the Glory gathering at Shekinah Regional Training Center, Doug kept hearing *The Great Awakening will bring people into the churches who have tattoos and piercings everywhere you can see and many places you should never see. There will be many who have soul ties beyond their numbering from recreational sex. Many have been addicted to so many substances they are now addicted to addiction. It is time for believers to quit being afraid of the devil and his demons and stand up in faith knowing the devil and his demons are afraid of them!"* With this word came two impressions: 1) We need to cast out the corporate spirit of the fear of the devil and demons. 2) God is waiting for the church to be ready to steward the Great Awakening so none will be lost as many were after the Jesus Movement. This preparation to steward the Awakening includes preparing a few from every church, or at least every city or neighborhood, to be thorough and effective in Deep Inner Healing and Deliverance.

One of Doug's greatest calls is to equip others to do the work of the ministry in Sturgis, Michiana (the southwest Michigan and Northern Indiana region Pam and I oversee for BAMN), and beyond through books and seminars. To that end Doug has launched regional "Equipping and Certification Programs" in Northern Indiana with Pastors Michael and Judy Peterson; in Eastern Michigan with Apostle Barbara Yoder, Pastor Benjamin Dietrich, and Deborah Combs, and West Michigan with Pastor Leigh Larson.

ABOUT PAMELA CARR

As you have seen in Pam's contribution to this book, Pam is an overcomer. She is also an incredible worship intercessor. She leads our church in interceding for God's will through worship.

Pam's greatest call is to release the Presence of God through personal and corporate worship. She is head of worship ministry and pastors His House Foursquare Church in Sturgis, beside her husband.

Pam assists as an intercessor for deliverance and deep inner healing appointments, and as a seer, she often sees things that set captives free.

Pam and Doug have a blended family with five children, twenty-four grandchildren, and fifteen great-grandchildren.

For more information on Doug and Pam's ministry and seminars or links to his books visit:
www.dougcarrfreedomministries.com

Other Titles by Dr. Douglas E. Carr:

Free Indeed ~ A Primer for Deliverance Ministry
Beat Me Up Spirits
Defining Moments – My Journey Toward the Kingdom
Free Indeed from Root Spirits

Getting to The Dirty Rotten Inner Core Series:
- *V.I: Anger, Frustration, Entitlement.*
- *V.II: Breaking the Octopus Grip of Addictions.*

Schematics: God's Blueprint versus Satan's Programming
God's Say So versus Man's Know So
Let's Get Real! Stepping into God's Reality
Kingdom Thoughts 101
Kingdom Thoughts 201
From Woe is Me to WOW is HE!
Choosing Kingdom

Busting Through to Greater Freedom:
Dethroning the Counterfeit Trinity.
Taking the Bite out of the "ites."

Ephesians for Deliverance Ministry:
Volume One: Building on a Sure Foundation

Of God, Gifts and Men Series:
- *Volume I: Motivational Charismata Gifts*
- *Volume II: Holy Spirit Manifestations Gifts*
- *Volume III: Ascension Gifts*

Making Abundance a Lifestyle Rather than an Event.

Coming soon: "All You Need for this Life ~ Seven Special Names of God.

CPSIA information can be obtained
at www.ICGtesting.com
Printed in the USA
BVHW031303040220
PP10635500001B/1

9 781973 684510